Fighting Back

Bob Steenlage

The Inspirational Story of Bob Steenlage

by Mike Chapman

Cover painting by Blair Jensen, professional painter.

FIGHTING BACK
THE BOB STEENLAGE STORY

Table of Contents

Continued on next page

These 2 Bob's Have in Common . . . (**Bob Hope & Bob Steen-lage**) . . . Bob's intimate encounter with a land mine field, snipers, booby traps and armies of rats . . . Bob & Bobbi's first-born **Eric**—a profile of faith, patience, and commitment.

DEDICATED TO
HOWARD S. "HOWIE" PONTUCK

All of us who knew him were priviledged and we miss him; and to the memory of all my West Point classmates who gave their lives for our country

Fred G. Bertolino
Arthur G. Bonifas
William D. Booth
David C. Brown
David R. Crocker, Jr.
Allen R. Culpepper
Peter F. Donnel
John A. Fera
Billy W. Flynn
Michael F. Grisafe, Jr.
Thomas J. Hayes, IV
Richard E. Hood, Jr.
John T. Hoskins
Gary D. Jackson
Charles F. Johnson

Donald R. Judd
Gordon T. Kimbrell, Jr.
Peter J. Lantz
Dennis D. Loftheim
Robert W. Luecki
Hugh R. McKibbin, Jr.
Frank Meszar, III
Martin K. Miskanen
Arthur M. Parker, III
Frank A. Rybicki, Jr.
Frank J. Schap, Jr.
Robert M. Snell
Louis R. Sustersio
Richard W. Thompson
David R. Wilson

ACKNOWLEDGMENTS

I would like to express special thanks to Mike and Bev Chapman for their "above the call of duty" work in preparing my story. Without them there would be no book. I would like to thank everyone who provided pictures, newspaper articles, and general information from my youth to the present. This list includes: Oma Chody Selle, Bob LeMar, Kent Townley, Jacki Fox Gordon, Jim and Connie Craig, Gene Guenther, Alan Perkins, LeRoy Alitz, Bob Kinney, Mike Caruso, Mark Scureman, Bob and Cindy Robbins, David Welsh, Laura Blobaum, Ron Seaman, Marie Steenlage and the Britt Chamber of Commerce, Dudley Markham, Tom Carhart, Gary Fowler, Art Nelson, Les Anderson, Jeff Smith, Britt News Tribune, and Harold Zook.

I want to thank my brother, Les, and my mother for all their help. I also want to thank my wife, Bobbi, our children, Eric, Keith, Sarah, Esther, Timothy, John, Barak and Ella for their inspiration. They were my driving force.

OFFICE OF THE GOVERNOR

STATE CAPITOL

DES MOINES, IOWA 50319

515 281-5211

TERRY E. BRANSTAD
GOVERNOR

September 9, 1993

To Whom It May Concern:

I have recently had the opportunity to become personally acquainted with Bob Steenlage. He has been a guest in the Governor's residence and we have had occasion to visit at length concerning his life experiences. I find him to be a man of great faith, integrity and wisdom. He has a very powerful message based on his personal experiences.

Bob has the ability to communicate with all ages. I have heard him give an excellent presentation to a group of adults and also witnessed a more personal conversation with my son. He is a man of compassion and understanding and he has the ability to really inspire and motivate people.

I am proud that Bob Steenlage is a native of Britt, Iowa, the first four year state high school wrestling champion, a graduate of West Point, a Vietnam Veteran, a teacher, farmer, and most of all a devoted husband and father of a large family.

I consider it a privilege to count Bob Steenlage as a friend and I highly recommend him as a motivational speaker.

Sincerely,

Terry E. Branstad
Governor of Iowa

FOREWORD

Robert Steenlage is a 1966 graduate of the United States Military Academy and a Vietnam veteran. He has an important message he is presenting to groups throughout the United States — a message predicated on his own experience as an abused and neglected son of an alcoholic father. (He has since forgiven his father.)

During those years, he faced many challenges to become the first four-time high school wrestling champion in the state of Iowa. He followed high school years by gaining admittance to the United States Military Academy at West Point; he met that challenge and is also one of the greatest wrestlers to come out of the Academy. It was rewarding to observe Bob struggle with academics, the Academy's system, and the demanding preparation necessary to be successful on the mat.

Following graduation from the Military Academy, he served in Vietnam and was one of the many veterans persecuted by certain factions upon his return for defending this country's commitment to freedom. It would have been so easy for him to turn to "the easier wrong," but the love of his family, his wife, and abiding faith have been his strengths.

Bob has the ability to communicate with people of all ages. Because of his faith and integrity, his love and concern for others are evident. Therefore, his message is a valid presentation in contrast to the artificial, self- serving messages we are exposed to through the media by great athletic performers and professional politicians.

It is my hope the readers of Bob's story will recognize that there is a little of his experiences in all of us. We all are capable of coping with adversities successfully if we recognize a higher power and are willing to make the necessary sacrifices. Also, I trust the readers will have a better understanding of the "Duty, Honor, Country" concept which is such an integral part of the development of the West Point graduate. In truth, this message is not only a tribute to Bob's commitment, but also to those many people who have influenced Bob in his struggle to emerge as the great American he is today.

LeRoy A. Alitz
Head Wrestling coach—West Point (1954–77)
Associate professor—West Point (1954–present)
National Wrestling Hall of Fame

CHAPTER

1

Standing in the wings of a high school auditorium, waiting to be introduced, Bob Steenlage felt the tension gnawing at him once again. As a professional speaker, he had been in this situation hundreds of times before during the past several years. It was a situation he should have been very accustomed to.

And yet, he was nervous. Very nervous. "I feel it every time I give a speech," said Bob, in his quiet manner, reflecting back on the moment, and others like it. "I always feel like I'm going to fail."

He pauses, and then continues. "Thinking I was a failure, and that I was going to fail at whatever I tried, was pounded into me, over and over, as a youth. Today, thirty years later, I still have to struggle with that negative self-image...."

A negative self image for Bob Steenlage? That's hard to imagine for those who are familiar with his story.

In 1962, he became the first high school athlete in the state of Iowa to win four state wrestling championships. Upon graduation from high school, he was selected for an appointment to United States Military Academy at West Point, New York, where he would have the opportunity to follow in the footsteps of men like Ulysses S. Grant, George Armstrong Custer, George Patton and Dwight David Eisenhower.

He graduated from West Point in 1966 and became a commissioned officer, serving with distinction in Vietnam.

Later, he taught school, coached, worked as a businessman and raised a wonderful family. By 1990, he had ventured into the competitive world of public speaking and had forged out a successful career; he was in demand all across the nation, speaking to educators, students, soldiers, businessmen and athletes.

By nearly anyone's definition, Bob Steenlage was a success at everything he tried. And yet, here, once again, waiting to address a group of high school students, thoughts of failure were attacking him like a swarm of killer bees.

The reason rests in his roots. Bob Steenlage grew up as the son of an alcoholic father.

Though his father never really abused him physically, he actually did much worse; he abused him emotionally by totally ignoring him. Neglected by his father, small and apparently unblessed with any talent or skills that might elevate him up and out of his poor and unfortunate family circumstances, Bob seemed at an early age doomed to accomplish very little with his life.

But there was a fire burning deep inside him. While he could do little to control his outer environment as a youth, he could control his inner world. As a skinny seventh grader, he made up his mind to become the first ever four- time state champion in Iowa, the wrestling hotbed of the nation, hoping such an accomplishment would earn him a full ride college scholarship. He was convinced education would be his salvation; through education, he felt he could rise up and overcome his situation.

The trouble was, hardly anybody else believed in his goal. In fact, nobody really knew about it except for his mother, grandmother and great aunt. He never talked about it until his senior year, when it became obvious. With the support of the three women in his life, he set out on his voyage, determined to make athletic history.

His hometown had spawned many great wrestlers through the decades, but in late February of 1962, Bob Steenlage stood alone at the top of the ladder. In fact, no athlete in the wrestling-crazy state of Iowa could match what Bob Steenlage had done. The skinny, quiet lad from a town of two thousand residents had become the very first to ever win four high school state wrestling championships in Iowa.

Against all odds, he became a cadet at West Point. The world seemed ripe for him. While the future seemed bright and full of hope, it was actually just the opposite. Despair and frustration lay just ahead.

Finally, Bob Steenlage dropped out of society. Awash in emotional pain, the Bob Steenlage of the 1960s was replaced by the Bob Steenlage of the 1970s and 1980s, and this Bob Steenlage was in trouble.

His life no longer had meaning, purpose, or direction. It seemed as though the bitter memories of his boyhood, combined with the unrelenting terrors of Vietnam and the travails of being a parent under siege, had taken a toll which could never be repaid.

But, somehow, he changed again. He came fighting back, determined to redeem himself, to emerge from the lost years, to reclaim his pride and his passion. He emerged slowly at first, picking his way carefully; and then with a vengeance, travelling the Midwest and, finally, the nation, to tell his amazing story of rebirth.

Bob Steenlage came fighting back. Overcoming all the obstacles fate had placed in his path, he resolved to become, once again, a winner in life.

This is his story.

CHAPTER

2

Shortly after the conclusion of the Civil War, a string of railroad stations popped up across the state of Iowa. In 1870, in west central Iowa, one of the stations was the start of a town, which became known as Britt, named for a now long forgotten employee of the Chicago, Milwaukee and St. Paul railroad.

Those who settled in Britt were rough and hardy by demand, for life in the prairie states of the 1870s and 1880s was anything but easy. Long, severe winters, prairie fires, disease and poverty were constant companions; but those who made a home out of places like Britt, Iowa, raised families that valued hard work and discipline.

John Robert Steenlage came into the world on February 28, 1944, the oldest of five children born to John Clarence (Jack) Steenlage and his wife, the former Evelyn Loy. Jack was born on a nearby farm in 1918, the year after the United States entered World War I. Some twenty years later, he was destined himself to fight in another world war, this one with a Roman numeral II attached to it. He saw action in Italy, and was wounded there. He was awarded the Purple Heart.

Evelyn Loy was an only child, and when her parents divorced, she had one goal: to get married and have children. Six years younger than John, she met him before he left for the war. They were married on May 5, 1943.

Les was born four years after Bob, followed by Jerry, Nancy and Cindy. Maybe the Steenlage family once had the potential for a Donna Reed style home life, or maybe it never had such an opportunity at all. Whatever its potential, the reality was miles removed from such a possibility.

"We had a tough life, and it seemed to me it was all because of my father," said Bob in the winter of 1992. "Maybe World War II and the injuries had some affect on him, I don't know. But he was a mean-spirited person to me. He was also kind of lazy, and I think he used drinking as a crutch.

"I didn't have any type of a relationship with him at all, other than when he came home drunk. It seems like there was always lots of yelling and screaming when he was home. And, in retrospect, it seems like he treated me the worst of all the children. Maybe it was because I was the first born."

The memory which haunts Bob the most is one of his father attacking his mother late one night. In a drunken rage, Jack threatened Bob's mother, and Bob, a skinny seventh grader of less than eighty pounds, rallied to his mother's defense.

"One night, it was particularly bad. Very bad. My brothers and sisters and I were all huddled upstairs, listening to him scream at my mom. We were afraid he was going to really hurt her. I went down the stairs and into the kitchen where they were. Without thinking, I grabbed a claw hammer out of the kitchen drawer and went after him with it.

"He threw me into the wall," said Bob. "I hit the wall so hard that it knocked the phone off the wall on the other side." Bob pauses, struggling with the memories. "I think that confrontation scared him, somehow, and I think it had an effect on him. I know it did on me...."

It was a memory that has stayed with Bob all of his life, through West Point and Vietnam, through coaching and teaching, through farming and raising his own family. It surfaces in long, lonely drives — and now, finally, in his talks.

Jack owned a tavern in Britt called the Hob Nob, and it's where he retreated for sustenance, of all kinds. He worked at the bar, socialized there, and drank there. He usually went off to work late in the afternoon, stayed until early in the morning, and came home night after night in a drunken stupor. He wasn't physically abusive very often, but there were enough times that Bob hasn't ever been able to completely escape the pain of the memories....

"We didn't have much. We were poor," said Bob. "He didn't work hard, and anything he earned I guess he spent, on booze or gambling. We just had enough to scrape by. My mother worked at the hot lunch room in school, and eventually became the head cleaning lady at the Britt Hospital. It wasn't a very happy life.

"My father had a yardstick made out of hickory, and he used to hit me with that. Not on a regular basis; only if he was in a foul mood and I got in his way."

One of his worst childhood experiences had only an indirect relation to his father's drinking problem. It was such a painful experience that Bob repressed the memory of it, for almost thirty years. It wasn't until the winter of 1991 that he was able to talk openly about it.

"When I was in seventh grade, a couple of senior boys trapped me in the hallway at school," he began, painfully recounting the details. "They were making fun of me,

because I was so skinny and because my father was an alcoholic. They called me names, like pencil."

He paused, as the memory came flooding back. "They
lifted me off the floor, and spun me around. I was scared,
I was so helpless. They were all about five years older
than me, and much bigger. One boy pulled out a yellow pencil, and held it up. Whenever I came down the hallway,
they would call me pencil, or say, `Here comes the alky-
pencil'.....referring to my dad being an alky, or alcoholic.

"It was a really traumatic moment for me, almost as bad as
Vietnam was. In fact, I never told anyone this story, not my
mother or my grandmother or any teachers, until just now.

"You know, people are secretly molested in many ways,
I've found out through hundreds of talks with students
today. It's a common experience, on different levels.

"It was certainly a very hurtful moment for me." But Bob
found ways to escape his unhappy childhood, if only for
summer respites. Though he was a city boy, he began hiring
out for farm work at the age of ten. The farm where he
worked the most was owned by Art Nelson, a hard working
farmer who had lost his wife-to-be in a plane crash several
years before Bob hired on.

"He treated me very well. He was someone to fill in a
father's role," said Bob. "I worked several summers for him,
and then three more summers at another farm, one owned
by the parents of my girlfriend, Jacki Fox.

"One of the reasons I liked to go to the Jerry Fox home was
because it was so nice to sit around a table, in a family atmosphere, with no shouting and yelling. I always felt inadequate in any type of social atmosphere. I was very shy and
insecure. I was looking for something to belong to, in the
absence of a real family life at home."

Farm work made Bob strong. Though lean, he was wiry
and had a powerful grip. He was also a competitor by
nature. And, alone in his room, late at night, he wasn't afraid

to dream. What he dreamed about most of all was finding a way to be someone, and to earn a college degree, so he could somehow, some day, leave Britt and its problems behind.

It was during these lean, hard years that Bob Steenlage discovered wrestling.

The sport of wrestling had its American origins in Vermont, coming to the Colonies in the 1600s with those men tough enough to gamble everything on a stake in the New World. Collar and elbow was the style employed along the Eastern Seaboard, named for the fact the wrestlers would begin each match by grabbing hold of the other wrestler's neck and elbow; it was a rough and tumble sport, much more combative than the refined Greco-Roman wrestling favored in Europe, where no holds were allowed below the waist and matches were often on the order of a chess match, the moves slow and calculated.

Americans preferred a wide open, rugged style, much like the country itself. The first great American wrestler of note was William Muldoon, who was the finest grappler in the Union camps of the Civil War. Wrestling was highly esteemed by the Union soldiers as a means of self defense and physical fitness, and, along with gambling, was the most popular diversion during the North-South conflict.

By 1910, wrestling was one of the most widely-followed sports in America, and the most popular champion was an Iowan named Frank Gotch. Born on a farm in Humboldt, just sixty miles west of Britt, Gotch was undisputed heavyweight champion of the world from 1908 until his retirement in 1913. Handsome and articulate, he once starred in a play which toured America and Europe, became wealthy in various business dealings, and was considered a top bet to run for governor of Iowa.

"As the idol of millions, Gotch made wrestling a big-time sport in his day," wrote Mac Davis in his book, 100 Greatest Sports Heroes. "As a matter of fact, he drew larger audiences than did the heavyweight champion of boxing. Babies had been named in his honor, as had buildings, toys, farm implements and a hundred other things. The word `Gotch' was a synonym for quality and strength."

In 1917, at the age of forty, Gotch was struck down by uremic poisoning, and died. But his legacy lived on. For decades after, young Iowa boys grew up dreaming about becoming another Frank Gotch. The state's tremendous wrestling tradition can be laid at the feet of Frank Gotch.

Britt, like many other Iowa farm communities, had a strong wrestling tradition by the time Bob was entering junior high. The team placed eighth at the Iowa State Tournament in 1951, crowning its first state champion when Dick Govig captured the 105-pound title. Britt moved up to fourth the following year, and Govig won his second title, this time at 112 pounds.

Ron Meleney claimed the 154-pound championship in 1954 as Britt finished third in the state meet, and the team was second in 1956, with titles from Chuck Conway at 127 pounds and Alan Hiscocks at 165 pounds. The little town of just over two thousand was somehow competing with the state's largest cities, and doing very well.

In 1957, Iowa split its high schools into two athletic classes, in an effort to provide smaller schools a better opportunity to compete. And in 1959, Bob Steenlage emerged on the scene for the first time. He had been dreaming of this season for several years, and had prepared for it in the best way he could.

"I wanted to get stronger, but I didn't have any money for weights," he said thirty years later. "With the help of Bill Peterson, my boyhood friend and classmate, and his father, Raymond Peterson, I made weights out of cement which I slid on a pipe and would lift down in the basement. I also bought a couple of old mattresses from a Britt merchant, and put them down in the basement to work out on.

"I would often sit in my room and dream about winning

big matches. I remember in the seventh grade I told my mother, grandmother and great aunt that I was going to become a ninth grade state champion and maybe win four state titles. I knew it had never been done before in Iowa, but I wanted to try and do it. I knew I had to do something really great if I was going to have any colleges interested in me. I never told anyone else of my goals; I thought they would laugh at me.

"My mom and grandmother just smiled, and said I could do it. I don't think they knew what it really meant, in terms of becoming a four-time state champion. But they were very supportive of me, and my dream, even though we never openly talked about it again."

Kent Townley was the Britt wrestling coach when Bob was a freshman. A former collegiate wrestler at Iowa State University, he competed in the 1956 Olympics in Melbourne, Australia as the 125.5-pound member of the Greco-Roman team. He had seen Bob wrestle on the junior high team, and knew there was raw potential in the skinny frame. But the trick would be to pull the toughness out of the young boy who was so timid off the mat.

Townley had taken the Britt job after serving one year as an assistant to Dr. Harold Nichols at Iowa State. Even in 1992, he could summon up vivid recollections of the job interview, and the importance of wrestling in the small Iowa community.

"The interview was hardly what I expected," said Townley. "The coach before me had been there just one year and was fired with a 4-7 record. I was told I had to win or else my longevity would be short.

"It didn't take too long into the wrestling season to see I had a lot of talented boys in both junior high and up through the sophomore class. Bob was one of those boys, and was in the eighth grade at the time. Whenever possible, I would schedule exhibition matches for Bob before our varsity meets. He was undefeated in junior high and also in his eighth grade exhibitions.

"Bob had an excellent work ethic, in the classroom as well as in the practice room. He set a good example for all the rest of the wrestlers as he was not a boaster, a showoff or loud-mouth, as many boys with his success would have been. I don't know whether it was my influence on the boys, or whether they were following the example set by Bob and other state champions on the team."

"I did lots of farm work and running to prepare me, but my biggest asset was my determination," said Bob. "I had to admit to myself from the very beginning that I was not a gifted wrestler. I honestly was only slightly better than aver-age, with a big heart. But, I also recognized that lack of ability did not have to be a hindrance, and shouldn't be dwelled on.

"I always wore the same wrestling shoes in the meets and tournaments. They were special shoes because they were given to me by Lennie and Betty Carter of Britt. Lennie had worn them as a high school wrestler in Osage after his mother had worked and saved to buy them for him. It always meant a lot to me that he gave me these shoes. They were black, made of leather, and looked like boxing shoes. In Lennie's later life I gave him the shoes back. After he passed away, the family gave me the shoes back."

Bob adopted a positive, "can do" attitude, and carried it on through each of his four seasons. He made the varsity lineup as a mere freshman, but lost twice during the season, once to Ron Jones, a tough wrestler from Iowa Falls.

Entering the tournaments at the end of the season, a single loss would spell the end of Bob's dream. But he scored three straight wins at the sectional meet, and advanced to the dis-trict tournament, where he scored three more wins.

Suddenly, as a raw freshman, he found himself at the State Tournament, on the campus of the State College of Iowa (now known as the University of Northern Iowa) in Cedar

Falls. He scored two more wins, and found himself in the championship finals, against Jones.

"I remember I heard a fan talking before the finals match," recalled Bob. "He said the wrestler from Britt could never beat Jones at 95 pounds, because the Britt kid was the skinniest kid he had ever seen."

Bob was skinny; but he was also committed, and focused. He emerged with a hard-fought 2-0 victory. He had won the state title as a freshman, one of just a handful to have ever done so in Iowa history.

"After winning it that year, I knew the only way to go was down," he said in 1992. "Mixed with the good feelings was great, great pressure. Some sportswriter said in an article that it was virtually impossible for anyone to win four state titles, because of the great wrestling around the state, the prospect of injuries and, of course, the pressure."

Bob played football all through junior and senior high school and as a sophomore earned a starting spot at outside linebacker on the varsity though weighing only 125 pounds. By the time wrestling season rolled around, he knew he could never make the 95-pound classification again, and he set his sights on winning a second state title, this time at 103 pounds.

But, there were complications....many of them, and painful ones. He soon developed cauliflower ears, a condition brought about when the ears are rubbed too hard, or hit just right. The ears swell with blood, and become extremely painful. Bob had to have his ears drained twice a week, a process that involves sticking needles into the ear to allow the blood to flow out.

"My sophomore year we wrapped my headgear in tape to hold it in place. In the semi-finals of the state tournament the tape slipped down around my neck, and I almost passed out," he said. "It was a long, tough and painful year for me."

As a state champion, he was a marked man all season

long. All his foes wanted a shot at the skinny kid from Britt, not convinced he had the skills and toughness to hold such a title as a mere sophomore. But what they found was a wrestler who never, ever gave up anything without a tooth and nail battle.

Bob complied a 19-1-2 record as a sophomore, proving that while very good, he wasn't unbeatable. But when the tournament season came around, he was in top form mentally. He never forgot his goal, and the declaration he made to his mother, grandmother and great aunt.

Once again, he battled to the finals of the state tournament. He won his second straight championship with a 4-0 triumph over Rich Leichtman, a talented scrapper from New Hampton who went on to star at Iowa State University.

With two state titles already in his pocket, Bob was halfway home to his goal. Yet, in some ways, the hardest part was yet to come.

"The pressure really began to mount my junior year," he said. "There were lots of rumors going around Britt. Some people were saying I was really stuck up, that I had become conceited. But that wasn't the case at all. I was still basically very shy, and I was still having the troubles at home with my dad. Even though I was doing well in sports and gained acceptance with my peers, I didn't feel like I was totally who I wanted to be."

Several of the teachers knew of the difficulties Bob was facing at home. Yet, with no reports of physical abuse, there was nothing they could do to help, other than provide friendship and support in after-school talks.

"Bob's home life left a lot to be desired, and I was well aware of the problems because we only lived across the street from his house," said Townley. "Sometimes after practice, I would sit in the wrestling room with the boys for as long as an hour to listen to their problems and give them counseling and advice. Bob was always there."

Bob LeMar was a teacher, counselor and assistant wrestling coach at Britt during Bob's last three years there, and coached Bob's younger brother, Les, in seventh and eighth grade. He was Bob's counselor during Bob's senior season, and still relishes the relationship they forged back then.

"Bob was a fascinating young man to follow," said LeMar, in 1992. "Usually, teachers, coaches, and counselors like to think their students learn a lot from them. In this situation, I learned far more from Bob than he ever learned from me. I use him as an example in working with young people to reach their goals. Bob would set an athletic or classroom goal — figure out what he would have to do (to work on) to reach this goal — then he would do it.

"Teachers loved having Bob in class. They couldn't believe such a great athlete could be so pleasant and such a hard worker in class. He was everything a teacher could ask for in a student.

"In his last three years of high school, I never heard him say a bad word about anyone. I never saw him angry. He was a model of student behavior.

"In my three years at Britt I saw Bob wrestle all his matches, but one (one of my son's was born that night). I never saw or met his dad — he never came to one wrestling meet. The only thing I heard about him was that he was a drunk."

The 1961 season, Bob's third on the varsity, was memorable for the entire school. For the first time ever, Britt won the state team championship. Britt scored 47 points to 37 for runnerup Jesup. One of Bob's best friends, Larry Lloyd, won the state title at 95 pounds, while Dennis Krull took the 145-pound championship. Dale Brcka finished second at 154 and Gerald Green took fourth at 103. Bob was first at 112, defeating Dan Sullivan of Corning in the finals by the score of 2-0. After three years, facing some of the stiffest high school competition in the entire nation, he had never lost in a post-season tournament.

At the end of the school year, Townley resigned as head wrestling coach, disappointed in the failure of the Britt school board to reward his efforts as head wrestling coach.

"If I have one regret in my life, it is that I always felt like I deserted the boys when we left Britt before Bob's senior year," he said in 1992. "After giving the school their first state championship, I was given the smallest raise in the four years of tenure. That wasn't the agreement when they hired me."

The man who replaced him was destined to also play a huge role in Bob's life. Jim Craig had been an NCAA champion at the University of Iowa in 1959, in the 177-pound class, and had the qualifications to become a top flight coach, on and off the mat.

"When I was first interviewed for the job, Bob's name came up almost immediately," said Craig over thirty years later. "A member of the school board wanted to know if I would try to change Bob's style if I was hired. I said no, I wouldn't change his style at all; I would try to help him perfect his own style.

"I got the job, and I could see right away Bob was a driven individual. He was also a 'people person,' but perhaps didn't even know it himself at that point in his life. If anyone on the team had a problem, Bob would find out about it and bring it to my attention, or to the attention of some other teacher. He was a very compassionate person, perhaps because he felt he was missing out on that at home, from his father. I don't know."

With three state titles behind him, Bob entered his senior season full of high hope. He was growing out of his shell, and was popular in school. Because of his work ethic, he was a leader in everything he tried: he was an Eagle Scout, started on the football team for the third straight season, and was voted senior class treasurer and student council representative for the senior class. In addition, he was named to the honor society, a terrific accomplishment because good grades, like wrestling, had not come easy for him. He had worked long, hard hours at his books, just like he had wrestling, in order to qualify for a college.

"Bob's senior year we had a new teacher come to the school named Ken Jensen," recalled LeMar in 1992. "Ken told me he knew we had a wrestler going for a fourth state title when he came. He said he had visions of Bob being a near animal, with hair coming out on all parts of his body and fire coming from his nostrils. He asked another teacher to point out this `monster' so he could see what he looked like. He said he was completely shocked. He told the other teacher, `You mean that pleasant, skinny, little kid with glasses, carrying all the books is the monster wrestler?' `Yep,' replied LeMar. `That's the guy.'"

"My greatest struggle actually came my senior year," said Bob. "The newspaper writers were putting a lot of pressure on me, and I felt a lot of pressure as the season got under way. There had never been a four-time state champion in Iowa, and Iowa was considered by many to be the best wrestling state in the entire country.

"Besides, I had two serious injuries to contend with. I seriously hurt my back in practice one day, going takedowns with Coach Craig. The doctor told me it was so badly injured that I would probably never be able to wrestle again. I didn't wrestle again for five weeks, not even in practice. I got back eight days before the tournaments, and wondered how would I ever get into shape in the short time I had left. Coach Craig had to be feeling the pressure also, since I had gotten hurt wrestling with him. But it wasn't his fault."

Bob barely made it through sectionals, winning his final match on riding time against an opponent he had pinned earlier in the season. At districts, the qualifying tournament for the state meet, it was the same.

In the first round of the state meet, Bob defeated Larry Bra-bill of Audubon, 7-1. His next match, in the semifinals, was against Osage's Ron Barker, who had scored a 9-8 victory over Bob during the regular season. "He was the best wrestler I ever faced in high school, and suddenly I was facing him again, in the semifinals of the state tournament. I hadn't been able to practice for a long time, and I wasn't in the best of shape. I fell behind in the early going, but somehow I managed to squeak out a 7-5 victory over him."

After that match, LeMar went to the coaches' hospitality room and wound up bragging to another coach about Bob's dramatic win over Barker. The other coach told LeMar, "Don't tell me about Steenlage: whatever it takes to win, he will do it!"

But the victory was not without cost. During the match, Bob suffered a separated shoulder. It popped out of the socket during the match, and was popped back in in time for him to resume. But the pain, both physically and mentally, was intense. He wasn't able to go to the hotel and relax or eat but had to stay in the practice room rolling around so the shoulder wouldn't tighten up. There, contemplating the final match of his high school career, Bob's mind wandered back to the vow he had made his mom and grandmother five long years earlier. He was so close to fulfillment, yet so far away.

He watched from the sidelines as Lloyd won his second state title, this time at 103 pounds, and pondered his own fate. Finally, the finalists were called for the 120-pound championship, and Bob took the mat, facing Steve Balsbaugh of Perry. A skilled and seasoned wrestler, Balsbaugh had plenty of incentive for an upset: not only was he going for his first state title, but he had the opportunity to be known as the man who stopped Britt's sensation from becoming the first four-time state champion in Iowa history.

"I felt like I was in a pressure cooker," Bob said of the finals. "It was a very tough match. My shoulder was hurting and he was wrestling very well. At the end of the match, we were tied 2-2 on the official scoreboard. The referee walked to the scorer's table to see if there was any riding time."

Riding time was computed by totaling the amount of time one wrestler controlled the other wrestler, to see if one had an advantage. If one wrestler had over 60 seconds time more than the other, he would be given an additional point.

"I knew I had ridden him longer than he had ridden me, but I didn't know if it was long enough," said Bob. "I watched the referee at the table; the crowd was roaring, because they didn't know what had happened, either. Then the referee walked back to us, and turned to me. He told me to take off my headgear, and I figured that meant I had lost.

"Then, he raised my hand, and said, `Congratulations, son. You had 61 seconds of riding time. That one second gives you one point son. You have just become the first ever four-time state wrestling champion.'"

The emotion of the moment was overpowering for Bob, and the 3,600 fans packed into the modest college arena on the campus of State College of Iowa in Cedar Falls. "It felt like a streak of electricity went from my feet to my head and back down again; then the tears started to flow," he said.

It was also a very emotional moment for his mother, Evelyn, and his grandmother, who had flown in from Chicago to see her grandson make history. "She was afraid of flying and knew almost nothing of wrestling, but yet she was there! That meant a lot to me," said Bob. "She was so tense during my match she kept covering her head with her coat!"

"I have to admit when he said he was going to win four states back in seventh grade, I didn't think he could do it," said Evelyn, in 1993. "After all, he was such a little guy. But Bob was always very, very determined to do what he set out to do.

"That last match, I was sitting with my mother. When Bob's shoulder popped out, we were so worried. My mother never showed much emotion, but about then I looked over at her, and she had a waterfall of tears on her face. I said, `Mom, what's wrong?' And she said, `Oh, he's never going to be able to do it now, with that shoulder like that.'

"But he did it, of course. And we were all so very proud of him."

Bob's grandmother wasn't the only one who had to contend with tears that night.

"I started crying again, thinking about the last six years, and all I had gone through," recalled Bob. "My teammates were all a bunch of rough and tough farm type kids, and when I looked at them, they all had had tears running down their cheeks. I walked over to my coach, and my teammates, and we began to leave the arena. Then, a runner came up to us, and told me to come back inside the arena.

"I walked back in, and everyone stood up. The public address announcer said that for the first time in the `history of the world' someone had won four state championships. They gave me a long standing ovation.

"I can remember thinking to myself, `Well, they won't be able to call me pencil anymore.'"

No one in the Iowa arena realized at the time that Mike Johnson, from Lock Haven, Pennsylvania, had become a four- time state champion just the year before. Ironically, Bob and Mike Johnson would face off against each other three years later in the finals of a major collegiate wrestling tournament.

For the second straight year, Britt won the team title, outscoring runnerup New Hampton by a 35-24 margin. Also earning all-state honors for the Eagles besides Bob and Lloyd were Gene Guenther, third at 133 pounds and Brcka, third at 165 pounds.

Bob's accomplishment was headline news in all the sports sections across the state of Iowa. Back in Britt, he and the team were met by a caravan of cars, and over 150 fans. He was named "Prep of the Week" by the Des Moines Register, the state's largest newspaper, the following week. In the column, writer Jim Moackler quoted Craig as saying it was Bob's devotion to the sport which brought him success; "He's driving all the time," said Craig. "He's a real student of the game....always knows just how he's going to whip his opponent. And he's a real stickler on controlling his weight."

When it was all over, Bob had compiled a record of 74 wins, seven losses and five ties. Nearly all of his setbacks had come when he was either injured, or wrestling up a weight class. But far more important than the overall record, of course, was the fact he had accomplished something no other wrestler had been able to do in the long, illustrious wrestling history of the state.

The end of the season marked a tremendous moment for Bob, his teammates, and his family. But not all of his family. While his mother had seen almost every match he had competed in during his remarkable and historic four year career, his father had seen very few of them and had offered almost no verbal encouragement or support. He missed the first three state tournaments Bob was in, but did see the fourth. Still, as far as Bob was concerned, there was virtually no support from his dad.

The fact that his father had seldom seen him wrestle led to a major confrontation during his final season. Bob came home from practice one night, and was met by his mother at the door. She told Bob his father was taking a photo of Bob down to the tavern, to hang on the wall.

"He was going to tell all his drunken friends how he made me a great wrestler," Bob recalled many years after the fact. Bob was furious to think the man who had given him almost no support through three long, gruelling seasons was now going to try and take credit for his successes, when it had been his grandmother and mother who had encouraged him every step of the way. He confronted his dad.

"I met him at the door that night, and asked him how he could dare do this to my mother," said Bob. "You're going to break her heart by putting up a picture of her son in that lousy bar.

"I looked him straight in the eye, and said, `I'm going to do whatever it takes to see that you don't put that picture up.' He pushed me aside, and mumbled something as he went out the door. But he never put that photo up."

After making Iowa athletic history, Bob didn't have long to bask in his glory. Just two days after the state meet, he was on a train to Ft. Leavenworth, Kansas, to take a written and physical test to see if he would be accepted to West Point. With his fourth state title and the separated shoulder still weighing heavily on his mind, he had to switch gears mentally somehow, and try and score high enough to be admitted. He was so scared he almost cried. He was worried about being able to do the required pushups and pullups because of his shoulder but wound up passing all the physical requirements.

"For years, people had been telling me I wasn't smart enough to get into college, and I believed them," he said. "But I wanted to go to West Point in the worst way. Leroy Alitz, the head wrestling coach there, was from Iowa, and had contacted me. He thought I was good enough to wrestle there, and I was determined to try and get in."

"In his senior year Bob worried constantly that his SAT scores were not good enough to get him into West Point," recalled LeMar. "But Bob spent more time, a lot more, on his studies and wrestling than other kids. Maybe this is part of the reason he accomplished goals that he didn't seem to have the ability to accomplish."

As much as he wanted to attend West Point, it wasn't his only alternative. When he had dared to dream of becoming a four-time state champion back in his lonely bedroom years earlier, he had figured it was a way to gain a college education. And he was correct. Letters poured in from college coaches around the country, offering scholarships — many of them full rides — to attend their schools.

"I had offers from most of the colleges in the Midwest," Bob recollected in 1992. "I took recruiting trips to the University of Michigan and Michigan State University, and to Minnesota. Also, Coach Townley was a graduate of Iowa State University, and he took me there several times, to see the campus.

"But Larry Lloyd and I agreed if I didn't get accepted to West Point, we would go the University of Minnesota together. We were both offered full rides there, and we thought we would go together, as a package."

Back home in Britt, Bob was a local hero after the state tournament of 1962. He was voted "most likely to succeed" by his senior classmates, but he wasn't convinced.

"Despite my successes, I didn't feel good underneath," he said. "I wanted very badly to make my mother proud of me, and to set a good example for my brothers and sisters. I was still full of self doubts, and felt very limited. I had hardly ever been taken to a public library, and had only left the county a few times.

"I didn't know anything about West Point until Coach (LeRoy) Alitz called me, but then I had never been to a state wrestling tournament until I wrestled in one my freshman year, either. I just knew one thing — I didn't want to be a bum, like I thought my father was.

"My mother made some mistakes while raising us, but gave us all the very best gift a parent can — love. She loved us through and through, and we all knew it. And my grandmother was beyond words. What she did for us, in my dad's absence of providing, was amazing. She took a job in Oak Park, Illinois, near Chicago, emptying bed pans in a nursing home. She lived in semi-poverty so she could send money home to us. She bought the house we lived in, and a new 1955 Chevrolet, not my dad. She paid for much of our food, and some of our clothes. And she flew to four state tournaments, just to see me compete. What she did for all of us is beyond measure."

There were others who were eager to help Bob along the way, as well. Teachers and coaches left a mark on him, and taught him the value of caring about others. They were qualities he would absorb and develop in himself.

"I had a teacher in eleventh grade tell me I would never be able to go to college because I was too slow," he recalled. "But when my math teacher, Oma Chody, found out, she went into a frenzy. She was furious. She said, `Don't listen to that kind of talk. You can do college work. You can do it.' When she spoke, I listened."

Bob passed his tests, and he was admitted to West Point, all expenses paid. When it came time for him to leave Britt, it was Oma Chody who drove him all the way from Britt to the state of New York, where West Point is located. In the winter of 1992, Oma Chody Selle wrote from her home in Downers Grove, Illinois, reflecting on her memories of Bob some thirty years previous.

"The first seven years of my career as a high school math teacher were spent in Britt," she recalled. "I went there in the fall of 1957 when Bob was in the eighth grade. Although I was a graduate of Iowa State Teachers College, which had a very strong wrestling program, I knew very little about the sport. How that was to change! Bob was not a student of mine that year, but I came to know who he was. He frequently wrestled exhibition matches prior to the start of the varsity meet. Even then he impressed people.

"The next year Bob was in my freshman algebra class. He completed four years of math in high school, and he was a student of mine for all of those math classes. I saw him struggle after football season to cut weight in preparation for the first meet of the season which, as I recall, was always the night before Thanksgiving.

"I remember how irritable the wrestlers were as they cut weight. This was about the only time I ever saw Bob in a bad mood, and he had lots of company. I also watched them after the wrestling season ended and they could once again eat as they wished. I compared their return to their natural weight to a tire being inflated.

"Bob was not an academically gifted student. He did not test well on standardized tests, and I did not put a lot of faith in their results. He was probably of average ability, but I don't remember what the test results indicated. What I do remember about Bob as a student is how hard he worked and how much he achieved. His work was always above average. Although Britt was a small school, there was a lot of competition. Bob worked hard and he achieved, both in academics and athletics. I was so proud when he was accepted at West Point.

"Over the years I have maintained contact with Bob. His wife Bobbi was also a friend of mine, but I can't claim credit for introducing them. I had left Britt by the time they met. I have visited them at Ft. Hood, Texas; Ft. Sheridan, Illinois and when they lived in Redwood Falls, Minnesota. It is always a morale builder to visit them, and I feel honored that I am a part of Bob's life."

There is no doubt Bob feels the same way about those educators who worked with him back in Britt.

"If I hadn't had teachers like Oma Chody, Kent Townley, Bob LeMar and Jim Craig, and my mother and grandmother to believe in me, I never would have made it," he said candidly, twenty five years after leaving Britt for a new world.

CHAPTER

3

How could an eighteen year old from tiny Britt, Iowa, hope to know what was in store for him when he enrolled on the campus of the world's most prestigious military college?

"The U.S. Military Academy was founded in 1802 by an Act of Congress to provide this nation both military specialists and engineers to carve out our expanding borders," wrote Joseph E. Dineen, in his book, The Illustrated History of Sports at the U.S. Military Academy. "West Point graduates served the United States well, building bridges, dams, canals, roads and railroads, in addition to defending our borders in defense of freedom and our democratic form of government."

West Point is situated on a high bank of the Hudson River, some fifty miles north of New York City. Its history runs rich and deep; it was the site of Revolutionary War forts which guarded the Hudson, an essential river for traffic flow. Among its graduates are two Presidents of the United States — Ulysses S. Grant and Dwight David Eisenhower — as well as such legendary figures as Robert E. Lee, John Pershing, Douglas MacArthur, Omar Bradley, William Westmoreland, and H. Norman Schwarzkopf.

Physical fitness has been an integral aspect of military training since ancient Greece, and the U.S. Military Academy has stressed athletic development since the turn of the century. The first wrestling coach at the Academy was Tom Jenkins, a rugged native of Ohio who was the professional heavyweight wrestling champion of America for nearly five years. Jenkins was so sure of his pugilistic abilities that he once openly challenged the great John L. Sullivan to a slugfest for Sullivan's world heavyweight boxing title.

Jenkins was born in Bedford, Ohio, in 1872, and by the age of twenty was earning his living as a professional wrestler. Standing five feet ten inches and weighing around 210 pounds at his peak, Jenkins was extremely powerful, and often carried a mean streak onto the mat.

Jenkins ruled supreme in American professional wrestling circles, back when the pro sport was legitimate, until he ran into Frank Gotch. Jenkins lost his American title to Gotch in a series of matches considered the most brutal in history. Shortly after losing the title, in 1908, he became wrestling and boxing instructor at West Point.

Idolized by most of the Cadets who learned self defense under him, Jenkins was a legendary figure on the campus. He retired in 1935, and was replaced as head wrestling coach by Lloyd Appleton, a native Iowan who was a silver medalist in the 1928 Olympics.

In 1954, another native Iowan, LeRoy Alitz, replaced Appleton as head coach. Alitz graduated from Iowa State Teachers College (now the University of Northern Iowa), after placing fourth in the NCAA tournament at 191 pounds in 1948. Because of his Iowa connections, Alitz had known of Bob for several years, and was anxious to bring him to West Point.

"When I first met Coach Alitz, I sensed he was a man who cared for me as a person, and not just as a wrestler," said Bob many years later. "I felt maybe he could become like a new father to me. And he lived up to that promise; he's a great man.

"He had coached at Osage High School, not far from Britt, for a while. In fact, I found out later he had been offered the Britt job at the same time he was looking at the Osage job, but decided on Osage because it paid three hundred dollars more a year.

"When I was a junior, he sent me letters which told all about the generals and great men who had attended West Point. He came to visit at our house, and I liked him immediately. He was so sincere and down to earth. I also met his wife and children, and they were a happy family, like I wanted to have someday."

Alitz invited Bob on a recruiting trip to West Point, and he saw the graduation of 1962's class, where the speaker was President John F. Kennedy. It was a trip and a weekend which Bob has never forgotten. Yet, there remained a critical dilemma to be resolved.

"I remember I asked Coach Alitz if he thought there was going to be a war in the coming years," said Bob. "I didn't like suffering and killing, and the idea of having to kill someone in wartime. He gave me an honest answer; he said based on what had happened in Korea, he didn't think our government would get itself involved in those types of situations again."

It was a prediction that came from the heart; and yet, it was one which was destined to fall far from the mark!

If Bob thought most of his problems were behind him once he left Britt and his father, he was mistaken. West Point turned out to be a gruelling, demanding experience. Never sure of himself academically, he struggled mightily all four years to stay eligible for athletics.

"In college, there were five major hurdles I had to overcome in life," said Bob. "The first was my father and the pain associated with our relationship. The second was the academic problems I faced, and the lack of culture I felt I possessed. Even though I was fifth in a graduating class of 49 at Britt, it was because I worked so hard, not because I was very smart. In fact, my test scores showed I wasn't a bright student, but was basically an overachiever, just like on the mats. At West Point, I was competing with the cream of the crop, the best students from schools all across the country.

"Third was my low self esteem. I was always feeling inadequate, and just couldn't shake that feeling. Fourth, was college itself; I almost flunked out four times at the Academy. In fact, I was in trouble almost every semester, from a grades standpoint.

"And fifth was wrestling. There was lots of pressure on me to do well, having been Iowa's only four-time state champion. I was convinced I was going to be an NCAA champ, but I knew there was a tremendous amount of hard work to be done if I was going to do that."

Few athletes train as hard as wrestlers do, and no other scholastic athletes face the mental torture of weight control, as do wrestlers. A football player, basketball player, swimmer or track athlete may be just as dedicated during the practice sessions, but when the practice is over they can usually relax at meal time, eating all they need or want. A wrestler, on the other hand, faces an ongoing battle with the scales, and the prospect of denying oneself water and food throughout most of a four-month long wrestling season can bring a wrestler to the breaking point. But such dedication can provide moments of humor, as well.

"It's hard for non-wrestlers to understand the discipline it takes to not eat after working hard all day in class and then in athletic practice," said Bob. "Imagine going to a huge mess hall at supper with 4,000 other cadets, and seeing all this marvelous food in front of you; everyone else is eating all they want, but you nibble at a salad, suck on a few ice cubes, and go home empty."

One incident regarding food, although not related to cutting weight specifically, has remained fresh in Bob's mind over twenty five years later.

"It was during my first two months at West Point, on a hot summer day, when the upper classmen could dictate what the plebes could and couldn't eat," he said. "It wasn't humorous at the time, but it sure seems funny when I look back on it. When I left the mess hall I grabbed an extra cup of ice cream and stuck in on my head, under my hat, to smuggle it out of the hall.

"I was walking quickly across campus to get to my room and enjoy the ice cream. But I was stopped by two upperclassmen, who wanted to talk. As I stood there in my uniform, I felt something running down my face. The ice cream on my head was melting, and streaming down my cheek. Fortunately, they never saw it," he said, with a chuckle.

Plebes are always subject to the whims of the upperclassmen and there was also the traditional aspect of training that goes along with any sort of "boot camp" military training, whether the training takes place at an educational institute or a drill station where raw recruits are sent. The toughest part for Bob his first year was the continual memorization that took place, and which had to be recited word for word when plebes were confronted by upperclassmen.

"There was so much we had to learn and memorize, especially the first year, as plebes," he recalled. "There was a whole book of information, called the Plebe Bible. When an upperclassman commanded you to do so, you had to recite long passages. I had never been a very good reader and wasn't very good at memorizing, so it was very difficult for me. Also, I had a hard time learning how to spit shine my shoes, which is an old military tradition. Many of my classmates were older and had been in the Army and so knew about spit shining; I had never even heard of the term before.

"There is also a philosophy to try and humiliate the plebes, to see if they will crack when following orders. It can get very demanding, and very tough to take."

Early in his freshman year, he was sought out by a group of upperclassmen who were interested in seeing, and testing, the four-time state wrestling champion from Iowa. They corralled him one evening, and made him hold his rifle at arm's length until his arms dropped from total fatigue. Then, they made him hold out a sword until his arms dropped again. Then, the same procedure was repeated, this time with a bayonet.

"They were laughing each time I dropped my arms. They thought it was great fun to make this wrestling fellow break under the strain. At the end, they made me hold out my arms, then dropped a pin in my hands. My arms dropped again, and they laughed even harder.

"But, it wasn't really so bad," he said. "It's just part of the indoctrination process."

He recalled another series of incidents which might have even led to his leaving West Point, had not his roommate stepped in. Mark Scureman, a fine wrestler from Kingston, Pennsylvania, became Bob's roommate his freshman year, and they became close friends. An upperclassman had taken a dislike to Bob, for no apparent reason, and was riding him hard. Bob felt tremendous pressure, and it was affecting his classroom performance. Mark found out about it, and went to a friend of his who was also an upperclassman, and the latter intervened. The harassment stopped, and Bob never forgot the favor Mark had done for him.

Ironically, Bob's college wrestling career was almost a complete reversal of his high school career. At Britt, he had lost at least one dual meet each of his four varsity seasons, but never lost once in the much more important season-ending tournaments.

During his four-year college career, Bob never lost a dual meet. It was in the tournaments where he experienced the most trouble.

An NCAA (National Collegiate Athletic Association) title is the primary goal of any collegiate wrestler. The NCAA tournament debuted in Ames, Iowa, in 1928, and quickly became the measuring stick of a college wrestler's career.

At the time Bob entered West Point, the Academy had seen just one wrestler — Mike Natvig, like Bob a native Iowan, claim an NCAA title. Natvig came from Decorah, Iowa, to win the 147-pound NCAA title back to back, in 1962 and 1963. Bob was determined to join Natvig on the very elite list of NCAA champions.

He made an impression with his teammates almost from the very beginning. Scureman and Bob Robbins, both destined to become All-Americans, weren't impressed with the skinny Iowan when they first saw him. But they soon felt quite differently.

"I wound up working out with him fairly soon our freshman year," said Scureman. "I didn't know anything about him, but he didn't look too impressive. When Coach Alitz paired us up, I thought I would try a good move or two and finish him off fairly quickly. Well, everything I tried went nowhere. I couldn't work anything on him. And his grip, it was like iron. I couldn't believe it. He was so good. When you wrestled him, it took all your energy, because he wouldn't stop going, every second. It was like having a tiger by the tail.

"After we got done working out, I went over to Robbins and said, `Hey, have you worked out with that guy yet?' Robbins just smiled and said, `Yeah, he's pretty good, isn't he?'"

In order to get to the NCAA tournament, wrestlers from around the nation had to earn a high place in various qualifying tournaments. The Army team had to qualify through the Eastern Intercollegiate Tournament, the oldest established tournament in the nation, and one of the toughest.

Though undefeated in dual meets as a sophomore, Bob had a tough Easterns. He placed third, high enough to qualify for the NCAA meet which was being held at Cornell University in Ithaca, New York. But he had undergone emergency appendectomy surgery in the middle of January, and wasn't able to compete at full strength the remainder of the season. At the NCAAs, he won his first two matches and then was eliminated with a loss.

As a junior, he was again unbeaten during the season, and won the Easterns with dramatic victories over two of the best 130-pounders in the country, Joe Peritore of Lehigh and Mike Johnson of the University of Pittsburgh. The Johnson match was a highlight because it pitted two four-time state champions against one another, maybe for the first time in national wrestling history. Johnson had won four prep titles in his native Pennsylvania, and was considered a favorite over Bob by many people.

"The truth is, everyone there expected Johnson to win," said Scureman. "He was a phenomenal wrestler in high school, winning four state titles. He was a year ahead of Bob, and I don't think he had ever been taken down in college. He's about all wrestling people out East were talking about.

"He and Bob went into this incredible match. It was classic textbook wrestling, non-stop action from start to finish. The place went crazy; I was up next, and I didn't even care. Johnson was my hero in high school, and here he is wrestling my best friend.

"Finally, Johnson goes ahead with just seconds left in the match. Bob needs a takedown to win, and Johnson hasn't given up a takedown for years! Suddenly, Bob hits him with this picture perfect takedown in the final seconds, and wins. The place went wild. I just stood there crying.

"I was up next, and Bob comes over to me and said, 'Mark, you better get out there.' I went out, but I didn't even seem to care. I lost to this guy I had beaten earlier in the season, and when my match was over I ran over to Bob and started talking about his match."

But what would turn out to be the most-talked about match of his college career took place earlier that season in a dual meet. Bob turned in one of the greatest performances in Cadet history when he encountered Mike Caruso, of Lehigh University.

Caruso had been undefeated during his prep high school career in New Jersey. At Lehigh, for many years a wrestling powerhouse, Caruso was considered to be an almost automatic three-time NCAA champion.

The Army-Lehigh wrestling showdown is one of the longest and most proudly maintained athletic traditions in the East. And the night Steenlage met Caruso won't soon be forgotten among diehard wrestling fans. The two met at 130 pounds in front of a sellout crowd of 4,500 wildly enthusiastic fans at the West Point fieldhouse. When the smoke cleared, Bob had won, 7-2.

Years later, a sportswriter who was covering that meet remembered someone had run in from the parking lot to tell him his car was on fire. "Let it burn," the reporter is rumored to have said. "Caruso is losing and history is being made." Caruso did lose, and the car burned.

At the time, no one could have guessed the loss to Bob would be the only setback in Caruso's three-year varsity career at Lehigh. Caruso would go on to become the Engineers' only three-time NCAA champion, and retire from competition with a 57-1 record in college.

The season finished quite differently for Caruso and Bob. At the 1965 NCAA tournament held at the University of

Wyoming in Laramie, Caruso won the 123-pound championship, while Bob failed to place. In fact, Bob was lucky to even arrive in Laramie.

"The Army was thinking about not sending us because of the cost," recalled Bob. "We went in a Piper cub plane, about four of us and the coach. We landed in Laramie in the middle of the night, and went to a local high school to work out and get our weight down."

Bob won his first two matches at 130 pounds, and then lost a close match to Michigan State star Don Behm, who would go on to place third. In 1968, Behm earned a silver medal at the 1968 Olympics in Mexico City at 125.5 pounds. Scureman, on the other hand, had a terrific tournament, and earned All-American honors by finishing third at 147 pounds. Robbins was also an All-American, finishing sixth at 137.

His senior year, Bob finished the dual season undefeated once again. In the Easterns, he lost on a very disputed call the 130-pound title he had won the year before.

"Some of the calls the referees made were bad," wrote columnist Lee Richards of the Union-Gazette in Port Jervis, N.J. "The worst call of the tourney had to be the two takedowns Army's Bob Steenlage did not get credit for during his bout with Joe Peritore of Lehigh.

"In the last call, Steenlage, came around behind for a sure two points and the win, as there were only seconds showing on the clock and he was trailing, 3-2. The two grapplers came off the mat a few feet in front of us. From where we were sitting, Steenlage had the two.

"But the referee seemed to choke on the call. Army coach LeRoy Alitz said, `He lacked integrity in making the call,' and said it was one of the worst he has had against a boy in many years.

"The call was so bad that Peritore of Lehigh, showing the man he is, told Steenlage, `You won the bout, I did not beat you.' He made the worst call in the tourney," concluded Richards, in his column. The coaches were so upset that they voted Bob second to Jim Nance (Syracuse's great All-American football player and NCAA heavyweight wrestling champion) in the outstanding wrestler award. The film showed Bob clearly had the winning takedown.

The 1966 NCAA tournament was held in Ames, Iowa, the site of the first NCAA meet thirty-eight years earlier. A total of 64 teams and 227 individuals were entered. The location, just ninety miles from Britt, meant that many of Bob's family and friends would be able to come watch as he faced his last opportunity to become an NCAA champion, or at least an All-American (back then, a wrestler had to place in the top six of his weight class to earn All-American honors).

Despite a badly sprained ankle, which the trainers taped like a cast, Bob felt good going into the meet. He was captain of the team, and was one of its acknowledged leaders. He had been competing at 130 pounds all season, but decided to drop to 123 pounds for the final tournament of his long career. Unfortunately, Caruso was also at that weight, and the two Eastern stars were on a collision course.

After the first two rounds of the tournament, it appeared Bob was indeed on his way to fulfilling his goal. He decisioned Richard Cortes of Adams State (Colorado) 9-0 in his opening match, then pitched a second shutout with a 5-0 triumph over Martin Little of Kansas State. In the third round, he faced one of the nation's best wrestlers in the University of Oklahoma's Bryan Rice, and won 5-2.

But Caruso was wrestling very well, too. He scored easy victories in his first three matches and was set to face the only man who had ever defeated him in college. It was then that fate seemed to step in, and deal Bob a crushing blow.

"Before my match with Rice, Myron Roderick, head coach at Oklahoma State University, came up to me and said he hoped I would beat Rice, to help his team win the title. I was told I had several hours before I wrestled again so I went back to the motel to rest.

"But after what seemed like just a short time, someone was beating on the motel door, shouting I had to go right away, that I was to be called in a matter of minutes. I barely got to the arena in time, and had to run right out to the match without getting warmed up. Mike hit me with a quick move, and suddenly I was behind 4-0 in the first few seconds, before I even knew what happened."

Bob had to play catch up for the remainder of the match. He was the aggressor, but couldn't quite catch the slick Caruso. When the nine-minute bout was over, Caruso had his revenge, by the score of 4-2.

Twenty-seven years later, Bob and Caruso met again in Lehigh, Pennsylvania, where Bob was giving a speech. The two old rivals had the opportunity to reminisce, and to get to know one another off the field of competition. It was a bitter-sweet moment for Bob, but he gained some satisfaction from Caruso's comments to newspaper writer Mark Wegryn, of The Glove-Times.

"I got all four points on one move, he was pretty much on top of me the rest of the match," Caruso told Wegryn. "Bob had to be the finest competitor and wrestler I ever came up against."

After the loss in the semifinals, Bob still had the goal of placing in his first NCAA tournament and gaining All-American status. To do that, he needed to win at least two matches in the wrestlebacks.

His first opponent in the wrestlebacks was Iowa State's Rich Leichtman, the same Leichtman he had defeated in the finals of the state tournament when he was a junior. Bob scored a 4-2 win, and then found himself facing Warren Crow, a tough battler from Albany State. The winner would be third in the NCAAs, while the loser would finish fourth.

Wrestling the last match of his entire career, Bob posted a 7-3 victory. He was, finally, an All-American!

Meanwhile, Caruso's teammate Peritore, who had beaten Bob on the controversial call at the Easterns, finished second at 130 pounds, falling in the finals to the great Yojiro Uetake of Oklahoma State, who never lost in his three- year college career. Perhaps if Bob had remained at 130, he would have been in the finals there.

Teamwise, Army tied for tenth in the nation, one of its best showings ever. Bob led the way with his third place finish, but Bob Robbins also scored valuable points by taking fifth at 145 pounds. That Army class of 1966 actually boasted three All-American wrestlers, as Scureman had finished third in the NCAAs the year before at 147 pounds. Scureman missed the entire 1966 season due to an injury suffered in an intramural football game.

"People often get the impression that wrestlers are these big, rough tough guys with no feelings," said Bob. "Well, during our senior season, all three of us went to a movie one day, just to relax. It was Walt Disney's `Bambi.' Bob Robbins was sitting in the middle, with Mark Scureman on one side and me on the other side. About halfway through, in this real sentimental part, Bob Robbins feels a tear running down his face. He's embarrassed about it, and turns to see if Mark Scureman has noticed it. He sees Mark Scureman has tears running down his face, and so he wipes his own tear away, and turns to me, so we can tease Mark Scureman — and here I am sobbing with tears running down my face. Three big tough All-American wrestlers, crying at `Bambi.'"

Bob had always shown compassion throughout his life, and often it manifested itself in a wrestling room. During his Britt days he had shown over and over his concern for the well being of teammates. It was a trait he continued to demonstrate through his West Point career.

Gary Fowler, a wrestler from Clearfield, Pennsylvania,

was one year behind Bob at West Point. In 1993, Fowler recalled the positive effect Bob had on him as he tried to adjust to West Point wrestling. Fowler said he was scared to death to come into wrestling practice as a freshman and was actually trembling as he walked into the room.

"But Bob must have sensed my fear," related Fowler. "He came over to me, put his arm around my shoulder and said, `you are now one of us. If there's anything I can do for you anytime, just let me know.'" Bob's concern erased a good deal of Fowler's fears about making the adjustment, and Fowler vowed then and there he would make every effort to pay back the kind deed if ever the occasion arose.

The loss to Caruso in the semifinals nagged at Bob for the next twenty seven years to such a degree that he felt, once again, he had failed. Despite making Iowa history and despite never losing a dual meet at West Point, he was disappointed with his wrestling career.

It took a letter from Bob Kinney, longtime sports information director at West point, written in 1993, to put his career in its proper perspective:

"Bob Steenlage is, without a doubt, the best Army wrestler I have ever had the privilege of watching in my thirty years serving the U. S. Military Academy in its sports information office. What impressed me the most about Bob, aside from his brilliance on the mat, was the manner in which he handled himself as a representative of the U. S. Military Academy — the way he responded to adversity, the positive influence he had on his teammates and those involved with the Army wrestling program.

"Bob didn't lose very many matches during his four years at West Point, yet when he did he was always gracious in defeat and quick to congratulate the winner. He also knew how to handle winning, and handle it well. A lot of athletes let success go to their heads and become somewhat aloof as a result. That wasn't Bob's way, though. He was always trying to improve, and always trying to help his teammates improve. I guess that's one reason why Army did so well during his three years competing on the varsity level."

Bob had lived up to the creed emblazoned on a huge statue on the West Point campus, words which had been spoken by General Douglas MacArthur back when he was superintendent there: "Upon the fields of friendly strife are sown the seeds that, upon other fields, on other days, will bear the fruits of victory."

Wrestling had been a big part of Bob's life at West Point, but certainly not the only important aspect. The institute provided him with a well rounded education and allowed him to meet a very diverse group of people. He learned a great deal about discipline, how to be an officer and a gentleman, and how other educated men and women felt about a wide variety of topics.

He also met, during his West Point years, the woman he was to marry and share the rest of his life with. He didn't meet her in West Point, but back home in Britt, Iowa, during a brief respite from his military existence.

Roberta (Bobbi) Goltz grew up in Waterville, Minnesota, one of three children in a family where turkey farming was the mainstay. It was, according to Bob, a good and traditional family life, far different than what he had experienced in Britt.

She graduated from Mankato State College, and began teaching school in Britt during the fall of 1963. Arriving the same year was Al DeLeon, another in a line of exceptional college athletes who came to coach wrestling at Britt. The Mankato State matman placed second in the NCAA at 130 pounds in 1962, the same year Bob won his fourth state title. The previous year, DeLeon had also earned All-American honors by finishing fourth at 130.

Bob returned to Britt during Christmas leave of his sophomore year at West Point, and met Bobbi at Stewart Wallace's, a mutual friend. They were introduced by Bob's very good friend, Gene Guenther, who had placed third in the state for Britt in 1962.

"We hit it off right away," recalled Bob. "We talked a lot that night, and I told her I had to go to Minneapolis in a couple of days to fly back to West Point. She offered to drive me up there since she was going to Minnesota anyway and I was really excited about that.

"At the airport, there I was alone with no family; just Bobbi and me. I wanted to hug her goodbye but I decided I shouldn't. We wrote for a long time, and grew very close through the letters, and during the few leaves I got.

"When I came home for two weeks that summer, that's when we began to realize this was serious. We wrote during my junior year and she decided to try and find a teaching job in New York so we could be closer to each other.

"Coach Alitz was concerned; he wanted to know if Bobbi's moving out here would hurt my wrestling. I said it would be just the opposite, that she would be a motivational factor for me to try and do better."

That she was. Bobbi became a strong supporter of not only Bob's, but the entire Army team. She would always drive down the highway behind the Army team bus in her little blue Nash Rambler, following it to its next meet or tournament. The military wouldn't let her ride on the team bus.

Bob and Bobbi were married in Waterville on June 16, 1966. It was just nine days after he graduated from West Point. Mark Scureman was best man and Bob's brother, Les, was groomsman. Twelve cadets drove all the way out from New York for the wedding. The cadets were all high spirited and in a mood to celebrate; they provided the town of Britt with some colorful entertainment during their brief stay.

Naturally, Bob and Bobbi were very excited about the future and what lay in store for them. Little did they know how much pain and turmoil the coming years would bring.

Upon returning from World War II in 1945 Bob's father Jack with Bob and his mother Evelyn.

The beginning—7th Grade 1957, weighing 75 lbs. and wearing his dyed long underwear, Bob sets his goal to be a state champion.

The new teacher at Britt asked to see Bob, this near animal, with hair all over, and fire coming from his nostrils. Instead he found a skinny, little kid with glasses, carrying a load of books down the hallway. This is the monster wrestler?

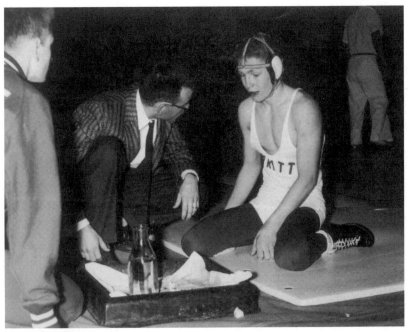

Getting instructions from Coach Townley against East Waterloo 1960, Gale Frank off to the left.

Britt's 1st undefeated dual meet season and Coach Townley gets a victory ride after Britt's win over East Waterloo. L to R: Dave Looney, Paul Peterson, Merlin Miller, Ted Conway, Coach Townley, Bob, Jim Nelson, Glenn Pitkin.

Oma Chody, Bob's math teacher in Britt. Oma greatly motivated Bob to reach his goals and later actually drove Bob to New York to attend West Point. Bob and Oma (Chody) Selle have remained close friends.

High School Football Fall 1961 Coach Steve Everett and outside linebacker, Bob Steenlage.

Britt's First State Championship Team 1961
1st Row L to R: Dale Brcka (2nd), Gerald Green (4th). 2nd
Row L to R: Dennis Krull (1st), Bob (1st), Larry Lloyd (1st),
Kent Townley, coach.

Britt's Wrestling Team 1962
1st Row L to R: Bill Formanek, Larry Lloyd, Gerald Green, Bob, Bill Peterson,
Gene Guenther. 2nd Row L to R: Les Steenlage, manager, Vinnie Kopacek, Gary
Kahlstorf, Alan Perkins, Coach Jim Craig, Dale Brcka, Glenn Pitkin, Robbie
Simpson, manager.

Britt's Second State Championship Team 1962
1st Row: Bob (1st), Bill Peterson state qualifier, Larry Lloyd (1st place). 2nd
Row: Dale Brcka (3rd place), Gene Guenther (3rd place), Jim Craig, coach.

ARMY

W
R
E
S
T
L
I
N
G

1964–65

UNITED STATES MILITARY ACADEMY
WEST POINT, N. Y.

Going to class at West
Point, U.S. Military
Academy 1965.

Bob on the cover of the West Point
Wrestling Schedule during his junior year.

1965 West Point Wrestling Team
1st Row L to R: Baily, Scureman, Sharkness, Abraham, Huyck, Arvin, Sepeta,
Steenlage, Fowler. 2nd Row L to R: Mgr. Paley, Mase, Carlson, Tucker,
Monroe, Keithly Wilson, Hanau, Schroeder, Fisher, Doogan, Asst. Coach
Powell, Coach Alitz, Robbins was absent. Bob Arvin was killed in Vietnam.
The West Point Gym is now Arvin Gym.

West Point Wrestling Team 1966
1st Row L to R: Ray Sepeta, Bert Fisher, Mike Baily, Bob, Bob Robbins, Mark
Scureman, Ken Schroeder. Back Row L to R: Coach Leroy Alitz, Roger
Heimann, Hugo Croft, Jim Harder, Russ Baker, Claude Johnson, Wayne
Monroe, Cooper Wright.

West Point parade, Fall 1965
L to R: Art Mosley, John Carrow, Bob, and Gaines Dyer.

West Point 1966
Bob in action against Penn State.

Easterns Tournament
Bob beating Mike Johnson, Pittsburgh U Mar '65. Two 4-time state (PA &IA)
champions meet on the mat. Bob wins 5–4 with a last second take down.

Easterns Tournament 1965
Bob receiving the 1st place silver bowl. L to R:
Weber, Penn State 4th; Joe Peritore, Lehigh 3rd;
Mike Johnson, Pitt U, 2nd; and Bob.

One of Bob's favorite pictures. Graduation from West Point, June 1966. First Row: Bob's mother Evelyn, Bob's grandmother Clara. 2nd Row: Mark Scureman (Bob's roommate), Bob. Background: Bert Fisher, wrestling teammate.

Bobbi during her first year of teaching at the Britt Schools. In 1963, the year Bob & Bobbi met.

Bob & Bobbi's wedding, 16 June '66
1st Row L to R: Cindy Steenlage, Linda Iverson, Paul Iverson, Judy Iverson
(Bobbi's nieces & nephew) Nancy Steenlage. 2nd Row L to R: Betty Ann Goltz,
Joanne Arnfeldt, Karen Iverson (Bobbi's sister), Bobbi, Bob, Mark Scureman,
Les Steenlage, Jerry Steenlage. 3rd Row L to R: Gary Isrealson, Bob Robbins,
Cooper Wright, Ken Carlson, Dale Brcka, Jim Beshey.

Bob & Bobbi's Wedding
Edward & Margaret Goltz (Bobbi's parents) Bobbi, Bob, Evelyn & Jack Steenlage.

After Bob & Bobbi's wedding. 1st Row L to R: Ken Carlson, Mark Scureman, Bob, Bob Robbins, Jim Beshey. 2nd Row L to R: Bob Taylor, Ken Schroeder, Gary Isrealson, Les Steenlage, Jerry Steenlage, Cal Larson. 3rd Row L to R: Neal Waddington, Dale Brcka, Cooper Wright, Ray Sepeta, unknown, Steve Hanau.

First one out: Airborne school 1966.

Steenlage family picture just before Bob went to Vietnam 1967 (Dec.). 1st Row: Bob's father Jack, Bob's mother Evelyn. 2nd Row: Jerry, Nancy, Cindy, Bob. 3rd Row: Les, Bobbi.

CHAPTER

4

"Theirs was the dream of all young men: to become heroes. Inspired by John F. Kennedy's call to serve the nation, the West Point class of 1966 first gathered above the Hudson River on a glorious afternoon in July 1962. But as the cadets swore their oath of allegiance, they could not begin to imagine the dark journey that lay ahead."

So reads the inside cover of the dust jacket for the book "The Long Gray Line: The American Journey of West Point's Class of 1966." Written by Rick Atkinson, a Pulitzer Prize winning journalist who is also a staff writer for the Washington Post, the book was published by Houghton Mifflin Company in 1989. The book's objective is to trace the class into and through the Vietnam War, where many members of the class perished, and where others were nearly destroyed on another realm of existence — the emotional plane.

No war in American history has been so divisive or so unpopular as the Vietnam War. As Atkinson wrote, none of the Cadets could have imagined the dark journey that lay before them. Certainly not Bob Steenlage.

During the early 1960s, hardly any high school student in the United States had heard of Vietnam, and certainly very few of them could identify it on a world map. Boys like Ron Kovic in Massatequa, New York, and Bob Steenlage in Britt, Iowa, were far more interested in wrestling and girls than in anything that had to do with the Mekong Delta or the Gulf of Tonkin.

But what Vietnam would come to mean to both Kovic, whose life story, Born on the Fourth of July, became a national rallying point for some in the late 1980s, and Bob was hard to imagine. Vietnam would change them both, and millions like them, forever.

Situated just below the massive land mass of China, and bordered between the South China Sea on one side and Cambodia and Laos on the other, Vietnam is a mere sliver of land. In terms of size, it's comparable to the State of Iowa.

The Vietnamese people are oriental, and closely related to the Chinese. Buddhism is the main religion, although there is a large Taoist population, and Confucianism is also prominent.

Vietnam is largely an agricultural country. The landscape, furnished with heavy rainfall year around, is lush and vibrant, with three-fifths of the cultivated land devoted to the production of rice. Sugar cane, corn, kapok, tobacco, tea and pepper are also prime products, as is rubber.

Small and militarily insignificant, the nation was often a pawn in the grip of other, more powerful nations. The French achieved a formal colonial dominion over Vietnam by a series of treaties in the late 1880s, and tried to maintain that control into the 1950s. During World War II, however, Japan took over the country and allowed a communist group known as the Vietminh to seize control.

The French and the Vietminh engaged in a long, bloody war for control of the divided nation. Peace was signed in

1954, and the nation was divided into north and south sections, two separate nations, as it were. The Communists gained control of the north, while the government in the south tolerated the western free market system. Shortly after, communist guerillas from the North, known as Vietcong, began attacks in the south.

The South Vietnamese government, continually wracked by internal power struggles, was unable to fight off the communist threat by itself, and pleaded for Western assistance. The United States, in its zeal to arrest the spread of communism anywhere in the world, answered the call, determined to keep communism confined to the north.

Matters came to a head when two United States warships were attacked in the Gulf on Tonkin in August, 1964, by North Vietnamese torpedo boats. The U.S. retaliated with air strikes on military installations in the north. Soon, the United States was entangled in what would prove to be the least popular overseas conflict in its history.

"The first time I ever heard the word `Vietnam' was in a classroom at West Point," recalled Bob. "I can just remember someone saying there was a war going on in a place called Vietnam, and some West Point graduates were being sent there. I certainly didn't realize then, of course, the impact that place would have on my life, and on the nation."

Graduation day at West Point was one of the finest moments of Bob's life. It was a beautiful, sunny day and the ceremonies were held in the football stadium. His entire family, even his father, came from Britt for the festivities; Bobbi and her parents were there, as well. And, Jim and Jeri Beshey, good friends from high school in Britt also came. Over 5,000 high school students had applied for admission to West Point the year Bob was appointed, and only 807 were selected. Of that 807, only 579 graduated....and Bob was one of them. The road had been long and tough, and Bob was proud he had managed to survive.

"People don't realize what you go through at a military academy," he said. "Beside the normal pressure of grades, there is the tremendous military orientation and discipline that you undergo. We couldn't call home for the first two months we were there as plebes, and no freshmen were allowed to go home for Christmas. Of course, the military academies have become more reasonable and many improvements have taken place the past two decades.

"I almost flunked out four different times. Almost all of the classes were taught by military people, and they were rigid and inflexible, for the most part. If you didn't get a passing grade, you still moved on with your classmates, and then you had one last chance to pass the subject by taking a four hour exam ten days later. One last chance, and that was it. If you flunked this test, you were gone — out of West Point, sent back home. There was no way to wiggle out of it. Some cadets had been known to commit suicide, the pressure was so intense.

"I had my toughest times with English, engineering and physics. On one occasion, two of my classmates, Brad Hartley and Cooper Wright, drilled me over and over and over for a final test, for hours and hours. When they were done, I was like a walking, talking physics encyclopedia. I went in and did so well on the test that the instructors pulled me in afterwards to quiz me. They figured I must have cheated, until they found out how well I had memorized the information. If you cheat at West Point, you get kicked out.

"Another time I failed a semester English class because I couldn't write or speak in front of people very well. Again, the pressure was enormous. But, an unusual thing happened; one of the English instructors, Major Nicholas Terzopoulos, kept me after class, showing a genuine concern and compassion about the upcoming four hour test which would determine whether I stayed in or was kicked out.

"He gave me some advice which I have never forgotten.

He said when writing you must always keep it simple. He said to follow three rules when writing: `(1) tell them what you are going to tell them, (2) then tell them that, and (3) then tell them what you told them.'

"As a result of his advice, I was able to organize my thoughts enough during the four hour exam to pass. It was another close call over getting kicked out. I have tried to find Major Terzopoulos to thank him today, but I haven't been able to locate him."

After graduation, Bob was sent to Airborne and Ranger School at Fort Benning, Georgia. The nine weeks of ranger training took place in Georgia and Florida at camps specializing in swamp and mountain terrain warfare.

"Ranger school was by far the most difficult physical and mental training I have ever experienced," Bob admits. "Ranger school was tough; anyone who has attended will say the same thing. Many do not graduate.

"Airborne school too was very difficult for me, because I have always had a fear of heights, even back in the days when I would throw hay bales in a hayloft on the farm," he said. "In order to graduate, I had to jump out of a plane five times.

"On the first jump, I was the commander of the group which went up. I was the only officer on the plane, a West Point graduate. I was supposed to be a leader, to set an example — and I was sitting there with my knees knocking.

"It took every bit of willpower I had to walk to that door the first time. But when I stared out the open door, and saw those tiny fields way down below, I couldn't make myself jump out.

"When the sergeant says `GO!' you're supposed to spring up like a grasshopper and leap out the door. He yelled it three times, and still I didn't go. And then he planted that big size 12 boot on my backside, and out I went.....

"Do you have any idea what it's like to get kicked out of

"Do you have any idea what it's like to get kicked out of an airplane? I remember thinking, `I hope I have a heart attack before I get smashed on the runway.'"

After surviving the first jump, Bob expected it would go smoother the second day, but it didn't. He froze again, and it got worse. He vomited. When his time came, he had to be shoved out the door again by the sergeant. The third day was a repeat. And the fourth day, it grew even worse; he actually crapped in his pants.

"The fifth time, I made myself jump," he said. There was even more training ahead. He was sent to Fort Monmouth, New Jersey, for six weeks of communications school. Then, it was Fort Hood, Texas, where he was made a platoon leader and later company commander.

In the summer of 1967, Bob received his orders: he was being sent to Vietnam, to serve in the signal corps with the 4th Infantry Division, headquartered out of Pleiku. Pleiku was located in the northern part of South Vietnam, known as the Central Highlands.

Staring down at the rich foliage of Vietnam from the relative safety of an incoming transport plane, he and the other American soldiers must have felt a shiver of anxiety. By December of 1967, there were an estimated one half million American troops in Vietnam and neighboring Laos and Cambodia, and the nightly television news and newspapers at home were full of frightening reports from the war-torn land.

Upon Bob's arrival in Vietnam on December 15, 1967, at the 4th Infantry Division he was assigned as an escort and communications officer for the upcoming Bob Hope USO tour. He was partially responsible for communications, security and the welfare of the troupe.

Only a year earlier, while a fresh-behind-the-ears second lieutenant, Bob had seen Hope up close and in person at the Ambassador Hotel in New York City.

"The father of my classmate, Steve Singer, was the President of the New York West Point Society. They were having a fund raising dinner for West Point at $100 a plate. A couple of people bought the tickets but said to give them to someone. As a result, two of us couples wound up with the tickets. It was a very big function at the Ambassador. At first people asked us to carry their bags as they thought we looked like porters in our dress blue army uniform.

"Here I was, just out of West Point and only four years out of Britt, Iowa, and standing in a huge hallway at the Ambassador when suddenly former President Eisenhower and his wife, Mamie, came walking down the corridor. We were dumbfounded; General Eisenhower stopped and said, `How are you men doing? Good to see you.' It was quite an experience. We stood there pressed against the wall just like we were cadets again being threatened by upperclassman.

"Bob Hope was the master of ceremonies at the dinner that night. Everyone besides us was either a president of a corporation, a colonel or a general!" Bob exclaims remembering back to the affair. The Vietnam association with Hope was quite an experience too, but from a far different perspective.

"The troupe's plane was almost shot down coming into Pleiku, which was the headquarters of the 4th Infantry," said Bob. "Two trailer houses were brought in by helicopter for Hope and his people to stay in. Racquel Welch, Barbara McNair and Les Brown and his band were the other big attractions. It was interesting to work with them, and see them, but it was also a very nervous time for me, not wanting anything to go wrong."

Despite continued threats of force from the Vietcong, the show went off without a serious incident. After two days, it was over; Hope and his troupe were gone, and Bob was about to be thrown fullscale into war.

On January 1, 1968, right after Bob Hope left, Bob was sent to a remote post just before the outbreak of the Tet Offensive, where one of the largest and most fierce battles of the entire war, was about to take place.

"It was a real hot spot," he said, the tension showing in his voice nearly twenty-five years later. "There were Vietcong all over the area. I had been sent out to take care of a management and morale problem; it was a small, isolated post. No one told me it was a high-level danger spot, and suddenly I was right in the middle of it.

"I arrived just before dark by helicopter. A few minutes before midnight, I woke up and saw flashes all around. It was almost like the Fourth of July. I rolled off the cot and grabbed my M-16 rifle. I heard lots of screaming, and knew there was killing going on, all around me."

It would have been anyone's worst nightmare. A suicide squad of Vietcong had invaded the small American outpost. Dressed in black pajama bottoms, stripped to the waist and their upper bodies smeared with dark grease, they were high on drugs, ready to die, and to kill, for their cause. Somehow, Bob survived the nightmare; when dawn broke, he found the other officer who shared his tent nearby, dead even though there were sand bags two feet high around the tent.

"I crawled out of the tent and saw carnage all over," said Bob, reliving the horrible day. "The first thing I saw was a Vietcong lying on the ground, with his brains flowing out of his skull. He had been shot with an M-16 just above his eyes. There had only been about fifteen of us there, and by morning there were only five of us left alive.

"I remember thinking as a kid I didn't like to see people shooting birds with B-B guns; how did I ever get myself into this mess?"

Bob was then made a platoon leader at Oasis, near Pleiku and then sent to Dak To. Shortly after his arrival at Dak To, the word circulated that two regiments of North Vietnamese Army (NVA) were planning to overrun the American post. Bob was out on his rounds, checking the five bunkers which fell under his command, when he literally walked into near disaster.

"Of course, I couldn't use a flashlight, as there were most likely Vietcong snipers in an advance patrol, just waiting outside the perimeter for an opportunity to pick us off. I was between the third and fourth bunker when a voice rang out."

It was a sergeant, challenging to see who was there. Bob responded appropriately; the sergeant asked for the password, and Bob correctly provided it.

"Then he told me not to move; he said I was in a live mine field."

The American commander at Dak To had expected the NVA to break through the outer perimeter of the post, and had instructed his munitions expert to lay mines on the ground. Somehow, the word had not filtered down to all the other officers, and Bob was caught squarely in a live mine field. At the time, he credited the training he learned in his early wrestling practices with saving his life.

"My first reaction was to run and get it over with, but then I remembered what my high school wrestling coach, Jim Craig, had always said about taking responsibility for the situation," said Bob in 1992. "Jim had told us `Do the best with what you've got at the time.'

"There was supposed to be a zig-zagging formation to the way the mines were put down, but of course I couldn't see anything in the dark. And I couldn't turn on the flashlight in case Viet Cong snipers were out there.

"I just stood there, unable to move, for a long time. I remember thinking, `This is it! I'm not going to make it.' And I found myself thinking of Bobbi, and how she would react when she heard I was killed in a mine field."

The sergeant, keeping his poise under the circumstances, told Bob to stay put and he would try and find the officer who had laid the mine field. He came back several minutes later, and was stuttering when he began to talk.

"He said, `Sir, there is nothing we can do until morning,'" recalled Bob. "`But you can't wait for then, because we could be overrun with NVA. You gotta get out of that field now, somehow....'

"I knew I couldn't stay there til dawn. I'd be out in the middle of nowhere with the NVA coming in all around me," said Bob. "And yet, I felt if I moved in any direction, I would probably step on a mine and be killed instantly."

Twenty-five years later, he had to pause and catch his breath before continuing.

"Finally, I told the sergeant to stand back, and three hours later found myself out of the mine field. The sergeant grabbed my arms and said, `Sir, I'm sure glad you made it!'"

Bob went to his tent, and collapsed on the cot, shaken to the core by the experience. But the biggest jolt was still ahead. The NVA attack didn't come for two more days, giving the demolition team time to go to the mine field early the next morning and check it out. After doing so, they showed up at Bob's tent, to meet the officer who had somehow, miraculously, avoided death.

"They looked at me, and shook their heads," recounted Bob. "They told me they figured the mines must have been all duds, or I wouldn't have made it. So, they began checking the mines where I had stepped. My footprints were solidly on three mines — and they checked out okay!

"`There was nothing wrong with those mines,' one of the sergeants told me. `They should have gone off the minute your foot came down on them.'"

After they left, Bob laid down on his cot, and the entire cot began shaking. It was too deep of a question to think about at the time, but later in life Bob would wonder why he was still alive. At the time, he blocked the question from his mind.

It was the biggest scare he would have in Vietnam, but not the only one. Months later, he was in the midst of a small convoy of jeeps returning from a foray deep into the jungle, in the heart of Vietcong territory.

"It was one of those really dangerous places," he said. "The convoy was moving along when suddenly we had a flat tire. We were near the end of the line, and the other trucks went around us, and just kept going. An officer normally isn't supposed to help with flat tires, but my driver and I looked at each other as the small convoy ahead of us began to disappear; then we jumped out of the truck, laid our weapons down and began to change that tire in record time.

"We worked side by side, as fast as we could go, not caring at all about any kind of rank. We just wanted to live. We worked without saying a word but wondering if a shot would ring out any second and get one of us. It was very hot and we were pouring sweat. The second the tire was fixed we were back in the truck and soon caught up with the others."

While Bob was fighting with all the courage he could summon up to survive the Vietnam nightmare, there were problems back home which would test his fortitude an equal degree. Bobbi was about to give birth to their first child, and she was writing daily to keep Bob posted of developments. Suddenly, at about the time the baby was expected, the letters stopped coming.

"I didn't know what was going on," Bob said. "They had agreed to send me a photo of the baby everyday from the newly invented Polaroid camera. I couldn't understand why I didn't receive any mail as the due date came and passed. Only later did I find out about the complications."

Bobbi gave birth to a son. However, there were problems with the delivery. Bobbi had many difficulties, and the doctors were worried she might not survive the birth. She did survive, but the baby was born with a cleft lip and palate. She had promised to send pictures to Bob every day but was hesitant because of the lip. They wanted to ask Bob to come for the operation but they figured the army wouldn't have allowed it. When Eric was two and a half weeks old, his lip was operated on without Bob there.

To make matters worse, just before Eric was three months old it was discovered he had no soft spot at the top of his head and his skull was completely grown together. A child's skull normally doesn't grow together until around seven years of age. This meant that when the brain grew it would push into the skull, causing severe brain damage. Bobbi and the other family members, who were heartbroken, simply didn't know how to write and tell Bob of the tragic news; they felt he had enough problems of his own in Vietnam.

The family held a meeting, with considerable crying and fretting. Bob's maternal grandmother, the same woman of indomitable spirit who had flown to all four state wrestling tournaments, finally stepped forward and took charge. She simply said, "Eric is going to have the operation and Bob is coming home. Notify the Red Cross, and they'll make it happen."

A decision was made for the operation on the baby at the University of Minnesota. The surgery was very dangerous. It meant cutting an opening in the top of the skull one and one half inches by seven inches and inserting a plastic membrane, which would allow the skull to expand as the brain grew. It was a dangerous operation because of the proximity to the brain and the loss of blood which always occurs in surgery of that nature. Naturally, Bobbi wanted Bob to be there.

"I was out in the middle of Vietnam when a helicopter landed," Bob recounted. "They had a message from the Red Cross, saying my son was in serious condition and that I was being sent home, to be with my wife and baby during the operation. I flew by helicopter to the base camp and from there got on a military transport to Cam Ranh Bay. Twenty minutes later, I was on my way home. First, we flew to Thailand, then to Hawaii, and then to California.

Fifteen minutes after arriving in California, I was on a plane to Minneapolis.

"Can you imagine the culture shock? Twenty six hours after leaving my weapons and the jungle behind in Vietnam, I was sitting in a waiting room of a hospital in Minneapolis, while a team of doctors was trying to save the life of our baby."

The doctors removed a strip of bone one inch wide and seven inches long from the baby's head. There was considerable loss of blood. The operation lasted over three hours.

The reunion at the hospital was bittersweet. The baby, who they named Eric, came through the operations fine. But Bobbi and Bob were warned by the doctors to protect the top of his head at all costs for the next ten years, until the skull had an opportunity to strengthen itself in the damaged area.

"It was so wonderful to be home, and to see Bobbi, Eric and my family," said Bob. "But, it was all over so fast, and I was soon on my way back to Vietnam. I can't explain the emotions I felt, leaving behind my family, my new baby, and everything I loved so much to go back to that place of fear and death and destruction.

"Going to Vietnam the first time, without knowing what was ahead, was bad enough; but going back to it when you knew what it was like was even worse." And one of the worst experiences cropped up shortly after his return.

"I was called into a briefing at 5 p.m. and simply told they were sending my company out on patrol, and I was in charge. I said okay, but I would need a couple of weeks to get the men ready as the men were trained only in communications, not infantry. Most of the soldiers were just raw, young recruits, and I wanted to indoctrinate them as best I could from my training experience at the various military schools I had attended. I wanted to give them every chance to stay alive out there. The Tet Offensive of 1968 was taking its toll and was the reason we were being sent on patrol.

"But the commander said we were to leave the very next

day at day break. I was shocked; this was about 5 p.m. I was up all night talking to the men under my command — showing them how to handle their weapons, and trying to make them aware of the danger, if they panicked, and of shooting their own men marching in front of them. My ranger school training proved to be invaluable; it saved lives!"

The next morning, the company of one hundred twenty soldiers loaded into helicopters and took off north, flying over hostile territory. Looking down at the dense jungles, with the scattered little villages of thatched huts every now and then, Bob now fully realized — for the first time — how very, very far he truly was from Britt, Iowa.

"All of a sudden, there we were.....myself and my company of men dropped off in the jungle, the remote jungle, and I was supposed to keep them alive and not get lost. I remembered getting lost in a one half mile square corn field on Gene Guenthers dad's farm near Britt. "When the helicopters took off to go back to the base camp, we were all alone," said Bob. "At first, when we set out on a reconnaissance patrol, the men were treating it like a hike in the woods. They were looking around and taking it all rather casually....until we got hit the first time. They then seemed to take everything seriously.

"Reality set in very quickly at that point." In Vietnam, there was almost constant fear of sniper fire, or of full scale combat. The prospect of death hovered over the land; it was almost something the men could smell. But, there was more to fear than just the Vietcong and their booby traps. A wide variety of large, poisonous snakes were common, as were other wild animals and poisonous shrubs. And then there were the rats....

One place we were at I was told about an army of rats which had moved through the area recently. Another soldier warned Bob there was good possibility the rats would come through the area again.

"Working around farms in the summer, I had seen plenty of rats," said Bob. "But nothing like this. Shortly after sunset, we heard them coming, moving through the underbrush. You wanted to do anything to get out of the path but you couldn't. There were thousands of them, a sea of rats, some as big as house cats. We had to make sure we had no food smell on our lips or fingers at night when we went to sleep or we would get bit. They were always sniffing to see if we were food they could eat. It was a sickening and scary feeling.

"A friend told me about the night the rats came through shortly after a brief but fierce battle with Vietcong. Several men were lying dead out in the brush. But it was too dark for anyone to venture out into the jungle to try and get the bodies in until daybreak. The next morning they found the gruesome scene of rats eating the bodies.

"Those are memories....which don't go away easily," said Bob quietly.

Probably few Vietnam veterans can recall any moments they would describe as pleasant. The only one Bob recalls was very brief, and came again in a rather isolated outpost. It involved General William Westmoreland, who had been named supreme commander in the Vietnam War in 1964.

"General Westmoreland was the superintendent of West Point my first two years there, and he came to several of the wrestling meets," said Bob. "One day, in the middle of the jungle four years later, I was at this small outpost and we received word by radio that the general was coming in. We all moaned and groaned, not in the mood to try and put on any fancy airs.

"When he arrived, all the officers, about fifteen lieutenants, captains, and a colonel, lined up. We were in combat gear, and it was very hot and muggy. Sweat was rolling down our faces and soaking our uniforms. I was about the seventh man in line; the general stopped and looked me in the face, and then glanced down at my name tag.

"Without hesitation, he said, `How did wrestling go your last two years at West Point?' I was dumbfounded that he could remember me after four years and all the soldiers he had met. We talked for just a moment, and then he moved on. But I was motivated to say the least — for about a day. It brought back memories and was a very pleasant diversion. But it didn't take long to get back to the reality of the situation."

Prior to enrolling at West Point, Bob had asked Coach Alitz if he thought there was any chance of a war breaking out in coming years. A kind, caring person and a pacifist by nature, he didn't even want to contemplate the thought of having to kill another human being.

And, as far as he knows, he didn't kill anyone in Vietnam. He knows he didn't do much shooting. Most of the time, he was on the radio, giving orders. He was seldom engaged in the day to day fighting, like the infantry was.

Yet, he knows the statistics from his class of 1966 are staggering. No class in West Point had as high a percentage of deaths in Vietnam as his class of 1966. One of every twenty was killed, and one of every six was wounded or maimed.

"Every few weeks now he got word of yet another classmate who died," wrote Atkinson, in his portrait of Tom Carhart, one of Bob's classmates, in The Long Gray Line. "John Hoskins, the rangy boxer from Louisiana who used to read Stephen Crane's poetry aloud in the barracks at West Point, was killed in the delta on an airboat. Shortly before his death, Hoskins had written his own eulogy:

> I am washed in the blood of my men;
> Their lifeless bodies I have lifted from the ground
> And carried in my arms...
> I am dead with them.
> I am washed with their lives."

Hoskins, the boxer, had eloquently stated the case for Steenlage, the wrestler...and for every one of his classmates who had fought in Vietnam. It wasn't necessarily the tough and the brave who survived this war; it was, rather, the fortunate. It wasn't raw courage and wrestling skills which enabled Bob Steenlage to escape the mine field. Just what it was would haunt Bob for years.

But the memories of war have always haunted soldiers trying to readjust to civilian life, probably as far back as the days of the Roman legions, under Caesar. And before. The fact is, war breeds the worst conditions that man will ever face — and uppermost is the constant, unyielding fear of death.

Novelist James Jones, who wrote <u>From Here to Eternity</u> and other top-selling books, didn't pull any punches when talking about war, and its psychological impact on the average soldier: "I went where I was told to go, and did what I was told to do, but no more." he said. "I was scared shitless just about all the time."

And there is more to contend with. "Poverty, privation and misery are the school of the good soldier," Napoleon once said.

Writing about World War II soldiers fighting in Sicily — where John Clarence (Jack) Steenlage had served — legendary war correspondent Ernie Pyle captured the lot of the common soldier more dramatically than even Napoleon: "The front line soldier I knew lived for months like an animal, and was a veteran in the cruel, fierce world of death. Everything was abnormal and unstable in his life. He was filthy dirty, ate if and when, slept on hard ground without cover. His clothes were greasy and he lived in a constant haze of dust, pestered by flies and heat, moving constantly, deprived of all things that once meant stability."

Jack Steenlage was most likely subjected to the very conditions which Pyle describes. If so, those conditions and the stark horror of war may have deeply affected his outlook on life, and set in motion the development of the qualities which made him despised by his eldest son.

"Jack used to have bad dreams once in a while," confided Bob's mother, Evelyn, while talking about her late husband in 1993. "He'd be rolling in the bed, screaming, and I'd have to wake him up. The bed would be shaking. You know, he said to me once, `They teach you in the Bible it's wrong to kill, and then they send you over there with a gun and tell you to kill someone.'

"He was in a foxhole once, in the front lines, I think in Italy somewhere. And another soldier fell in on top of him. I don't know if he was dead, or what. But that really bothered Jack. He had bad stomach problems after that. I guess maybe the war bothered him, just like it did our son Bob, many years later."

In his brilliant book, <u>No Name on the Bullet</u>, which is a biography of Audie Murphy, Don Graham, professor of English and American Literature at the University of Texas, makes the point by quoting a World War II veteran:

"Harold Bond, who served in Italy, feared what might happen to those inured to the hard life of the combat soldier: `He and men like him would have to give and give and give; perhaps they would have to give so much that never again would they be good for anything even if they did live through the war.' Audie expressed similar fears in his book and in many interview statements long after the war was over."

Eventually, war effects most of its participants in the fashion described by Harold Bond. It changes their lives, usually forever. Maybe that's what happened to Jack Steenlage. He may have left whatever potential for loving and caring he once possessed on a battlefield in faraway Italy.

There is little doubting the impact war had on Glenn Morris. Born and raised in tiny Simla, Colorado, Morris was a three-sport star at Colorado A&M (now Colorado State University), in Fort Collins. In 1936, he dazzled the huge crowds at Berlin Stadium as he won the gold medal in the gruelling decathlon.

In 1938, he played the lead role in "Tarzan The Fearless," and in 1940 he was an end for the Detroit Lions of the National Football League. Glenn Morris had it all, until World War II reared its ugly head. He enlisted, became an officer, and served as a beach master throughout the South Pacific Theater. He would land on a beach and direct the troops, often sending them to horrible deaths.

After the war, he could never fit in. He drifted from job to job, in and out of Veterans Hospitals, apparently suffering from some form of nervous disorder. In 1972, he died at the age of sixty-two, divorced twice, with no children and little money.

"I think the war changed him," said his brother, John, in 1990. "Glenn was never the same after the war."

That's what war can do to people. And when the war is perceived as useless or senseless — as the Vietnam War was by many Americans who fought there — the frustration can be overpowering, with no hope of escape.

"They wrote in the old days that it is sweet and fitting to die for one's country," wrote Ernest Hemingway, in 1935, between two world wars. "But in modern war there is nothing sweet nor fitting in your dying. You will die like a dog for no good reason."

Many men are willing to die for freedom, for country and for family. Not many are willing to die for no good reason. Was Vietnam a good reason? The answer lies deep within each individual.

CHAPTER

5

In the town square of Britt stands a large and impressive monument, dedicated to its citizens who gave their lives for the cause of freedom. Twenty-six names are inscribed there, including nine who died in World War I, thirteen who died in World War II, and two who lost their lives in the Korean War. Two men — Robert Olson and Keith Kahlstorf, four years behind Bob in high school and a wrestler in same class with Bob's brother Les — died in the jungles of Vietnam.

Bob Steenlage did not die in Vietnam. He came back to the United States, only to face two other battles: one was external, the other internal. But the latter took a heavy emotional toll on him, and caused him to re-evaluate what his life, or any life, is all about.

"So many had died from our class of 1966," said Bob. "I felt I should have died in the mine field, and could have died several other times. I wondered why I was spared, why I was the lucky one to come home. Howie Pontuck, my good friend, was killed by a mine. He was captain of the gymnastics team and I was captain of the wrestling team and we would often meet in the gym. He was one of the most tremendous people I have known."

The question, "why was I spared," is one soldiers have struggled with for decades, if not centuries. It was certainly a question which haunted the most decorated soldier in American history. Audie Murphy entered World War II in 1941 as a scrawny, one hundred and twelve pound eighteen year old from a tiny town in rural Texas. He survived some of the most horrifying experiences imaginable, and emerged at war's end with a total of thirty-seven medals, including the Congressional Medal of Honor. He became an instant celebrity when his photo appeared on the cover of Life Magazine, and he rode triumphantly into Hollywood, where he starred in over fifty movies.

But late in life, Murphy seemed to have a death wish. He couldn't understand why he had not been killed in Europe, when over 90 percent of his original boot camp unit had been either killed or seriously wounded.

When called a hero at one point late in his life, Murphy shot back that the real heroes were buried in Europe. He often had nightmares, reliving major battles.

Like Audie Murphy, Bob felt guilty about surviving the war. But that guilt was only half the battle he had to endure. The other battle came from Americans he encountered back home — Americans who hated the war, and everything about it.

"I'll never forget getting off a plane in California," said Bob, measuring his words. "I was there along with a soldier in a wheelchair. A group of men and women carrying signs against the war approached us in the airport, and asked if we were just coming back from Vietnam. When we said yes, they spit in our faces, and called us names like `babykiller.' Some of the protesters were sticking their fingers down their throats, making themselves gag, until they vomited into plastic bags and then threw it at us.

"I never wanted to go to war; I never wanted to kill anyone, let alone a helpless baby," said Bob, emotion in his voice even twenty-five years after the ordeal. But I had graduated from West Point; it was my duty to go, and I did. It was a very hard thing to bear, the death and destruction.

"Vietnam was a very troubling experience and so was what happened to us when we came home. All I wanted was to forget about the war, and be with my wife and children."

Once he had thought of a military career. But when his tour of duty in Vietnam expired, so did any feelings Bob may have had for the military life. He wanted to walk away from the military, and never look back.

Unfortunately, the second part wasn't that simple, as he and thousands of Vietnam veterans — famous men like Ron Kovic and Oliver Stone, and the others, less famous — would discover in the years ahead. The trauma of that ugly experience simply wouldn't let go.

Upon returning from Vietnam, he was stationed at 5th Army Headquarters, Fort Sheridan, Illinois, with a Top Secret clearance in communications. His specific job duty as a captain was to be in charge of all communications equipment for 5th Army Headquarters.

"I took over my post in the middle of January, 1969, at midnight on a Saturday night," said Bob, in the summer of 1992. "One minute after I took over, a drunk ran into the main power post — and all the electricity went out all over the post. The reserve generators did not go on like they were supposed to, and, as a result, the entire 5th Army Headquarters was without any communications. This was during the Vietnam War, of course, and was a very serious matter. I got chewed out for forty-five minutes by a general who had battle ribbons on his uniform that went from his neck to his waist. I found out later he had received a battlefield commission during World War II. All I could say was `Yes sir,' and `No excuse sir!' I thought I was a cadet at West Point again."

Bob's four year commitment to the Army was due to expire June of 1970, and he had made up his mind to leave the Army. Because of the war, however, the Army was not letting regular Army soldiers out when their time commitment was up. Later Congress reversed their decision and declared all those who had completed their military obligation time would be released. This situation delayed Bob's discharge causing him to have to serve two additional months.

"I wanted to get out so bad I could hardly wait," said Bob. The big day came on August 8, 1970. The thrill he had felt upon being admitted to West Point eight years earlier was dwarfed by the exhilaration of severing his ties with the military. He now felt like he was free at last, and could begin life anew.

After serving his time in Vietnam, Bob was transferred to the States, and was attending night school at Roosevelt University in Chicago trying to complete his masters degree in education. He had decided to join Bobbi in the teaching field once his discharge came through.

Bob and Bobbi's second child, Keith, arrived on the scene on April 15, 1970, without any of the complications which Eric had encountered. So, the Steenlages moved to Redwood Falls, Minnesota, anxious to see what civilian life would offer. Bob became a science teacher and head wrestling coach, while Bobbi stayed home with their two young boys.

Just when it seemed life might return to normal, the family was struck by another calamity. They were driving to visit Jim and Jeri Beshey some miles away from Redwood Falls when they saw a car heading straight for them. Bob made a split second decision to swerve off the highway to avoid a sure collision; but the driver of the other car, who turned out to be drunk, did the same.

They both turned back onto the highway at the last second. There was an awful mashing of metal as the two cars met nearly head-on.

"The motor of our car was pushed back into the seats," said Bob. "Eric was thrown from Bobbi's arms by the impact....and flew into the front window. His head, which we had tried so hard to protect ever since the surgery, struck the windshield so hard it broke the windshield out."

Miraculously, Bob and Bobbi escaped with minor injuries. But Eric was rushed to the hospital. For a period of time that seemed like days to Bob and Bobbi, they waited desperately for a doctors' report on their son. When the doctors finally emerged, they told the Steenlages there was a good chance their son would suffer some form of permanent brain damage.

"They also said there was no sense in running up a large bill, that there was nothing they could do for him at the hospital that we couldn't do at home," said Bob. "We took Eric home, and every single night, for three years, he would say `Good bye' instead of `good night' when we put him to bed. It was like he knew he was very badly hurt, and just might not be around the next day. It was heartbreaking to hear such a little boy say that...

"Every fifteen minutes or so at night, for three years, we would try to check up on him," said Bob. "Bobbi was suffering from a severe allergy attack much of the time, and at one point I thought she might die from fatigue and lack of sleep."

Little Eric was sick quite often, and for some time the scar on his head was quite visible. But as the years passed, he grew out of the sick stage, and began to prosper. The Steenlages had somehow survived yet another catastrophe in their lives.

"I don't know where we found the strength to get through it all," said Bobbi. "The accident with Eric was so devastating I thought I was going to have a mental breakdown. I would find myself standing in a corner sometimes, and crying. I was on the edge. I was taking some medication to get me through those times."

Alcohol, the most destructive drug in America today, had re-entered Bob's life to bring more tragedy. One of every ten cars an American driver meets is being driven by someone who is under the influence of some kind of drug. In colleges alone, students spend 5.5 billion dollars a year on alcohol. According to the 1991 college alcohol survey, 70 percent of administrators said alcohol is a major contributor to campus violence and is a factor in 40 percent of academic problems. Also, alcohol is involved in 90 percent of campus rapes. In fact, alcohol is involved in the majority of all home domestic problems. A study reported in the Journal of American Medical Association, based on data from the 1990 U. S. Census for the National Center for Health Statistics, says an estimated seven million U. S. children live with an alcoholic parent, and 18.1 percent of U. S. adults report having lived with an alcoholic or problem drinker when they were children.

Bob's wrestling team compiled a 10-2 record his first year of coaching and tied for the conference title. The next two years, Bob's teams were just average. Meanwhile, he had begun a part-time career as a distributor with Amway Corporation, and was doing well in that area, as well. In 1973, he quit teaching and went fulltime with Amway.

"I had five goals when I graduated from high school," recalled Bob. "One, I wanted to go to a good college. Two, I wanted to marry a good looking woman. Three, I wanted to have two children, which was the American dream back then in the sixties. Four, I wanted to have a nice home in the ritzy part of town. And five, I wanted to be wealthy.

"These goals now seem ridiculous but were based on my narrow perspective of life at the time.

"By the time I was twenty seven, I had realized those goals, to some degree. But reaching these goals didn't satisfy me. I was having nightmares over Vietnam, Eric was having his troubles, and we were getting restless. I just wasn't satisfied with my life."

He accepted Jesus Christ as his Lord and Saviour on January 3, 1973. Bobbi followed soon after.

"I was troubled," he said, reflecting back on that period. "I had gone to different ministers, preachers, in search of something. I even thought about committing suicide, but not seriously. I didn't want to shoot myself, and don't think I ever would have. I even wrote to Billy Graham; but I didn't get any answers from religion. No one seemed to have time for me.

"I went to the spare bedroom, read some Bible verses given to me by Wayne and Nancy Haapoja, and prayed. I was sobbing. Lightning didn't strike the room, the house didn't shake, or anything like that. But the next morning I could tell I had changed. I felt much better inside.

"But I was still twenty seven years old, had two children.....and I still hated my dad.

"I made the decision to drive to Britt, about a four-hour drive south of Redwood. My conscience was bothering me and there were a few things I needed to take care of. I went to find the owner of the Ben Franklin store in town, to pay for something I had stolen as a youngster for which I had carried a guilt with me all these years."

And then, he confronted his father. "He was sitting at the kitchen table when I went into the house. I walked up to him and told him some things were bothering me from the past, and I wanted to make some sort of peace with them, and him. It only took about two or three minutes. I told him I forgave him, but I'm not even sure he knew what I meant."

As quick as that, it was over. It didn't really change anything, but Bob was able to at least remove some of the pain by taking action of some sort.

Not long after that, on March 29, 1973, Jack Steenlage died.

He had been working at the bar, and collapsed behind the counter after closing for the night. He had suffered a fatal heart attack and was found lying on the floor.

"My mother called, and told me he had died that morning," said Bob, remembering the moment. "I felt nothing at all, less than if I had been told one of the farm animals had died. I acted serious for my mother's sake, and went through the motions. I didn't want to cause a scene."

Bob's parents divorced four and one half years before Jack's death and his mother had remarried. Leroy Stalzer was a bachelor farmer near Britt for many years before meeting and marrying Evelyn in 1972. They live in the house the family grew up in. Bob is happy for his mother, and enjoys a nice relationship with Leroy.

On November 30, 1975, Bob and Bobbi had another baby, their first daughter — but not without tremendous suffering. The doctor was expecting serious problems, and told Bob there was a chance the baby would be born dead, or that Bobbi would not make it through the delivery. In addition, a major snowstorm hit the area the night Bobbi was expected to deliver, so the doctor came to town and stayed overnight so he wouldn't be stopped from coming in.

Sarah almost died in the delivery room from lack of oxygen and Bobbi from hemorrhaging. Sarah was suffering from placenta previa so severely that her oxygen was being cut off. She was transferred to the Children's Hospital in the Twin Cities and declared well a week later. By early 1977, Bob, who had been through many major adjustments in his life, was looking for yet another.

"I wanted to change my lifestyle," he recalled. "I wanted to get out of the rut and the rat race; teaching school and working Amway just weren't what I was looking for any more. I always had good memories of the farm, back from my summers working in Britt. I wanted to be around animals, be out in the woods more.

"We were looking for five acres with a nice home; we ended up with one hundred and eleven acres, with a farm house that was not in very good condition." A year later they bought the adjoining 213 acre farm for a total of 324 acres.

The farm is situated in the rolling hills near Galesville, Wisconsin, just a few miles from LaCrosse. He threw himself into farm work as hard as he had attacked wrestling fifteen years earlier, in Britt. Perhaps, he thought, the key to his happiness could be found in good, long, hard, honest labor.

Just before moving to the farm, on July 1, 1977, their fourth child arrived. It was another girl, and they named her Esther. There were no complications at birth. Esther was followed by three more children — Timothy on February 5, 1979; John on April 15, 1980, and Barak, on November 1, 1981.

The farm work was hard, and not too profitable. Land values nosedived soon after they bought the farms. Still, they worked the land, trying to make ends meet and pull ahead.

On May 30, 1983, tragedy struck again. Bob and Bobbi's eighth child, Obediah, was born on that day healthy and robust at birth, but later developing a rare viral pneumonia at the age of seven months. They rushed him to the emergency room of the LaCrosse Hospital, concerned but confident he would be okay with professional treatment.

"We were sitting in the waiting room, thinking everything was going to be fine," said Bob, his voice subdued. "After several hours, the doctor came out and said they had done all they could, but they just couldn't save him. We were shattered."

They buried young Obediah on a gently sloping hill on the farm. And they threw themselves into their work, more determined than ever to work away the pain.

Their third daughter, Ella, was born on August 2, 1984, strong and healthy. Just when they were convinced nothing else could happen of a serious nature, it did. On January 1, 1985, a severe wind storm partially knocked over an old elm tree. Bob went out to saw the tree next to it, not realizing the elm was ready to fall. The sawing caused such a vibration that part of the elm tree collapsed on top of him. The heavy wood struck him on the head and his back, and he fell unconscious to the ground.

"I must have been out about fifteen minutes," he related. "Eric was with me the whole time, and brought me around. I was taken to the emergency room in LaCrosse right away. My pelvis bone was mutilated, and something was wrong with my spine. The cut on my head was dangerously close to the brain.

"One of the doctors told Bobbi I wasn't going to make it. But they couldn't figure out why I didn't go into shock. I heard them saying that to her.

"I remember telling Bobbi it wasn't my time. But even the slightest movement caused excruciating pain all over. They didn't want to move me, but I insisted they send me to Mayo Clinic in Rochester, Minnesota. I was convinced I would get the care I needed in there."

Once again, the fighter in Bob emerged. They inserted a screw in his pelvis to help hold the pelvis bone in place. Ten days after the surgery, they told him he might never walk again. He was in constant pain, and they were giving him drugs to fight the pain. Even though the drugs were helping to alleviate the pain, Bob made the decision to quit taking them because he felt he was getting hooked on them.

He went home in a wheelchair, almost unable to move. He couldn't walk from June 1 to August 21, and the pain was excruciating at all times. They wanted to do another surgery, but the pain got much better after a couple of months. His recovery progressed slowly. By the early fall, he was walking, although he tripped sometimes. He made up his mind to go back into teaching, to help pay some of the many bills that were starting to pile up.

He took a job teaching math and science at Gilmanton,

some thirty eight miles north of the farm. He taught for nine months of the school year, commuting, and continued working the farm, with the help of his growing boys.

But the tragedies continued almost non-stop. Another baby daughter came into the world on July 26, 1986. But Deborah was born with very serious medical problems. She underwent two critical surgeries in the first forty-eight hours of her life, and wasn't allowed to go home until she was almost four months old. She had to live in an oxygen tent one hundred percent of her life. On February 8, 1987, her little body gave out; she lies next to Obediah.

Only a mere eighteen months after Bob's accident, a mishap on the farm could have cost the life of their son, John.

Bob and his sons, Keith, sixteen at the time, and John, six, were baling hay on a hill when Bob saw storm clouds forming in the distance. Fearing it would rain soon with their work only partially done, he tried to beat the storm by driving faster.

"I was driving the tractor, with Keith and John on the hayrack behind," said Bob. "I was going too fast, the hayrack was bouncing around, and John fell off.....in front of the left wheel of the hayrack. Keith screamed at me to stop, but I couldn't hear him.

"The front left wheel of the hayrack ran over John's back; Keith was screaming `Stop! Stop!' but I couldn't hear him. Then Keith reacting quickly, leaped off the hayrack and grabbed John's shoulders and pulled him out of the path, just as the rear wheel was nearing him. If that wheel of the hayrack would have gone over him, with the added weight of the hay in the back....he could have been paralyzed, or died.

"I just went to pieces thinking how foolish I had been driving fast just to get some hay baled."

Bob paused during the retelling, fighting for composure. "I just couldn't have taken that. Probably one hundred yards from where this took place are the graves of our two children. I asked myself, `How could I be so stupid? Why are these things happening to us? How can this be?'"

The pain and the torment were indescribable. The Steenlage family had gone through enough tragedy.

Still, after all he had gone through, Bob Steenlage was facing one more change in his life. This one would be a donnybrook, and would take all the courage he could summon up. And yet, it would be a healing change, one which would not only help to heal the fires burning inside him and in his family, but the painful fires burning in others, as well.

CHAPTER

6

For so many veterans of Vietnam, the agony of those years and the memory of those horrible experiences simply won't die gracefully. They have lingered for twenty-five years, locked away in the deep recesses of the mind; when they finally erupt out into the open, the pain they bring with them is often excruciating. From the lowliest private to the highest commanders, the Vietnam impact was the same.

"He was a very young man when he went to Vietnam, but he returned an older man," said the sister of General H. Norman Schwarzkopf, in TV Guide. "He brought home a chestful of medals for his bravery, but none were enough to deflect the pain of what he'd seen, or the frosty reception that greeted him upon his return." Schwarzkopf, a 1956 graduate of West Point was a member of the wrestling team while a cadet, and in 1991 was the Allied Coalition Commander of Operation Desert Storm in the Persian Gulf War against Iraq.

America has fought in eleven wars, from the Indian wars of the 1700s to the Persian Gulf War. The greatest loss of American life came when American fought American; 618,000 killed in the Civil War. The second greatest loss of life occurred during World War II, with 353,000 killed; third is World War I, with 82,000 killed; Vietnam is fourth on the list, with 58,000 dead.

But how many more American veterans were mortally wounded psychologically? According to a June 14, 1991, report on the popular television show 20/20, the numbers are numbing.

"Every major conflict has coined its own name for the psychological trauma inflicted by warfare," said correspondent Tom Jarrel. "By the Second World War it became `shell shock.' It now has a medical-sounding term, PTSD, post traumatic stress syndrome. It's a huge problem. A recent comprehensive VA study of post-traumatic stress disorder pointed that out. Of the three million men who served in Vietnam, more than one half have suffered with problems, of emotional disorders, marital abuse, inability to hold a job. One in ten is homeless."

And then the final blow: "Nearly half a million Vietnam-era vets suffer from PTSD."

Bob Steenlage was one who suffered. The memories of Vietnam have haunted him ever since the first day there, back in 1967. And his wife, Bobbi, admits for years she wasn't sure what was the best way to help him overcome the pain.

"Not long after he first went over, one of my best friends back home lost her husband in the Vietnam War," she recalled. "He was supposed to arrive home on a certain day, and he did. In a box. I went to the funeral with her; it was very hard. All I could think was, `Will this happen to me?'

"When Bob came home, I decided not to talk about Vietnam at all, not to bring it up. I wanted to put it behind us, to forget about it. A couple of years ago, after he began opening up about Vietnam, he told me he resented the fact that I had never asked him about Vietnam, and what he went through. He had wanted to talk about it, but hadn't wanted to bring it up."

Now, Bob talks about Vietnam freely, almost with a vengeance. It's as if he is convinced the best way to deal with the memories is to get them out in the open, to confront the memories as if they are an opponent to be taken down and pinned. It's also the same way he has elected to confront the painful memories of his alcoholic father, and the neglect he felt from Jack Steenlage.

When a friend compared Bob's trials to those of Job in the Bible, who was struck with a series of cruel afflictions in the form of a test from God, Bob rejected that premise.

"I wouldn't want to be compared to Job in any way," he said quietly. "He was a righteous man."

For several years after the two accidents on the farm — the one which nearly crippled him and the hayrack accident which might have taken John from them — Bob pondered the direction his life had taken. He began to deeply explore his most private feelings, and to re-evaluate his life to that point.

"I think he felt like he was a failure in many ways," said Bobbi. "He was searching for a way to try and explain it all, to himself and to others, still wanting to succeed desperately."

Suddenly a turning point in his life began on May 15, 1989. For several years some of the students at the school where he was teaching had been asking him to give a talk on Vietnam, and he kept politely declining. He just couldn't bring himself to talk about the experience.

"But a student came up to me one day and looked me straight in the eyes and said, `You owe it to this generation to speak about Vietnam, so we don't make those same mistakes again.'

"That was a powerful argument. My heart melted, so I agreed to do it. Bobbi was substitute teaching that day, so she was about to hear this for the first time also. I stood up to talk and got out just one sentence, and then started crying. They waited for me; it took a couple of minutes, and then I went on. The speech was videotaped, and copies were made for my mother and Bobbi's parents. I thought they might better understand us after watching it.

"Soon other people were calling, and asking me to talk about Vietnam. Then, someone asked me to speak about substance abuse of all kinds, and everything began to change."

In August of 1988 Bob met Dudley Markham, who joined the Gilmanton School District that year after spending ten years in the military, graduate school and work. Bob and Markham developed a friendship over the next three years and Markham played a substantial role in Bob's emergence as a public speaker.

"I was there when Bob first spoke to those students in May of 1989," said Markham. "I saw the healing begin. As he spoke to his first audiences, we would spend time together assessing and evaluating his public speaking. This was an interesting process in that here were two, everyday ordinary people who were struggling together to improve Bob's delivery and speech content.

"Although we were quite green or inexperienced in this process, I feel that we were setting the stage for `The Bob Steenlage Story.' I believe this time period was critical for Bob because it was the beginning of a transition from teaching to a motivational speaker."

Bob began, for the first time, to emerge from his shell, and to talk openly with friends about how he felt. He questioned his feelings on Vietnam and on his early life; he questioned his values, even asking if it was worth working so hard to win four states wrestling titles in high school. He sought advice from a select few close associates, including his brother, Les, Assistant Athletic Director at the University of Iowa.

Slowly, the idea of speaking out to others about his life began to take form. Perhaps if he was so troubled, then others may be, as well, he reasoned. Perhaps if talking about his pain would help to relieve it, perhaps that same avenue of expression would provide a door of opportunity for others to do likewise.

But the prospect of speaking before large crowds was unnerving to him. He had never, even during his teaching days, felt totally comfortable facing large groups as a speaker. After spending the last few years on the farm and teaching at a small school, he did not relish the idea of doing this. But the prospect was intriguing and it kept coming back to haunt him, over and over.

"I remember Bob called me several times to discuss the possibility of going out to speak publicly," said a friend in the newspaper profession. "He had lots of reservations, as would most people. He wasn't sure anyone would care about his story. But I told him he did indeed have a very strong story to tell. In the newspaper business, we are always looking for unusual stories with a powerful message, and Bob's story certainly qualified on both counts.

"Then, there was the fear of opening up his life to others. But I told him true courage isn't the absence of fear, it's the conquering of fear. I knew he could conquer the fear with little difficulty, once he was convinced it was the right path to take."

The decision to go out and speak to others and tell his story wasn't easy. It took months of agonizing. After he decided to forge ahead, he began tentatively. But soon he was totally committed, pouring the same energy and unquenchable spirit into this new enterprise that he had poured into wrestling and studying at Britt, and West Point. While the anxiety prior to going on stage was often intense and very stressful, the release of pent-up emotions while speaking proved to be therapeutic.

For a year and a half, he tried to work in the speaking engagements with the farm and the teaching, combining the two. But as word spread of his message, the offers began to mushroom and the positive reinforcement he began to receive was overwhelming.

"Some kids came to me with tears in their eyes after the talks," he related in 1991. "So many of them. A young girl from one school told me she had thought of killing herself the very day I spoke, but after hearing the talk she felt she had found hope. She saw how I was able to cope with the problems, and it encouraged her to do the same. She has written me several times since I spoke at her school, two years ago. What a feeling it is to hear from her, and to find out she's doing well."

Similar stories poured in, and not only from the students. Teachers of all ages, some from dysfunctional families who had suppressed damaged psyches for decades, sought him out after talks, most of them with tears in their eyes. And tough, seasoned veterans of wars — all wars — lined up to talk privately with him. Many times after school presentations he was sought out by students searching for hope and encouragement. The principals of the schools often had to step in and break up the sessions to keep the school day running smoothly. The outpouring caught Bob by surprise, but convinced him more than ever he was now on the right path.

Finally, the speech requests grew so dramatically that he was confronted with a tough choice, of far-reaching ramifications. He was missing so much time from school, on the road, that his administrators wanted a decision from him — either commit to the classroom fulltime, or resign. It was a difficult decision, one he struggled with for weeks. He discussed the decision with Bobbi and close friends. He didn't want to desert his students but felt, on the other hand, there was a sea of young people around the country who needed to be encouraged. Yet, he had to think about his family and the insurance (dental and health) he would be giving up if he left his teaching position. He would also be giving up the security blanket of a steady teaching salary while working only on commission as a speaker. He also couldn't forget he had almost flunked out of West Point twice in English class because he had such difficulty writing and speaking well.

Convinced he had a message which could have a positive influence on the lives of others, he finally made the decision to give up his teaching position.

"I always believed if there is a conflict between heart and mind, follow your heart," said Bob. "Sometimes this gets scary but it is always worthwhile. If your motive in any venture is to help or benefit someone, you can never go wrong. Be a chance taker — that's the American dream.

"'It is only with the heart that the mind sees clearly,' said Antoine de Saint-Exutery, a French writer," Bob relates.

"Really, the decision to start talking about my problems was a natural outgrowth of my philosophy. Take one step forward; do something poorly until you learn how to do it well. That's what my whole life has been about. This philosophy takes away the word `failure' and starts `action,' which is vital.

"There are only two reasons anyone can fail in America: either they don't start or try to begin with, or they quit and give up too easily. One day, one month, one year, one decade or two decades too early. I got back from Vietnam on December 15, 1968, and could not talk about my alcoholic father or Vietnam until May of 1989......that's twenty three years!

"Now I feel I am forty nine years young."

Pleiku, Vietnam Dec. 1967. Bob's first assignment in Vietnam put him in charge of communications for the Bob Hope show. Thousands of troops in the background behind Bob Hope.

Vietnam 1968. Bob greets a Vietnam monkey.

Pleiku, Vietnam 1968. Bob on patrol.

Pleiku, Vietnam 1968. Bob showing some Vietnamese children the monkey.

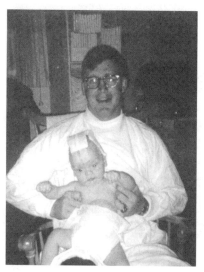

When son Eric had to have surgery at the age of 3 months, Bob was given an emergency leave to come home from Vietnam.

Central Highlands Vietnam 1968 near Pleiku. Bob, on the radio, during a patrol.

Pleiku, Vietnam Dec. 1968. Bob, Cooper Wright, Bert Fisher.

Vietnam. Bob and his platoon Sergeant at Oasis, near Pleiki. 4th Infantry Division.

Four-star General William Westmoreland, commander in Vietnam from 1964–1968 talking to Bob and others during the Tet Offensive of 1968. General Westmoreland had been the Superintendent at West Point, 62–64, Bob's 1st 2 years.

At Jim & Connie Craig's after Bob was back from Vietnam. Larry Lloyd, Oma Chody, Jim Craig, Connie Craig, Bob.

Bob & Eric at Ft. Sheridan after Bob's return from Vietnam. Airborne/Ranger 1969.

The children with Granny (Bob's grandmother Clara). 1st Row L to R: Timothy, John, Barak, Eric, Keith, Sarah, Esther, and Granny holding Ella 1985.

Bob on top of hill overlooking the farm 1988.

At home on the farm Bob and Bobbi with their eight children and friends, summer 1991.

Leheigh's three time NCAA wrestling champion Mike Caruso standing in front of his office with his secretary and Bob in 1990. Mike's only collegiate loss was to Bob in 1964.

West Point 1991 Standing in front of the All-American wrestling awards: Son Eric, Bob, and Senator Bob Robbins.

During one of Bob's east coast speaking trips Bob and son Keith visited the Vietnam Memorial at Washington D.C.

Bob at the Vietnam Memorial, Washington D.C.

New calf on the farm! Clockwise Timothy, John, Barak, Sarah & Ella.

The children with their sheep, summer 1992.

On the farm, 1992, clockwise from top left: Eric, Keith, John, Timothy, Bob, sister-in-law Connie Goltz, Ella, Sarah, Esther, and Barak.

On the farm, Bob with youngest daughter Ella and the fawn they rescued.

Bob visits his West Point wrestling coach Leroy Alitz and his wife Verda in 1991. Coach Alitz is still an associate Professor of Physical Education at West Point in 1993. He was elected in the National Wrestling Hall of Fame in 1992.

A banquet at West Point in April 1992 honoring Coach Alitz's election to the National Wrestling Hall of Fame brought many of Bob's West Point wrestling teammates together. 1st Row L to R: Cooper Wright, Bob, Ken Carlson, Gary Fowler. 2nd Row L to R: Bob Robbins, Ray Sepeta, Claude Johnson, Neils Biamon, Tom Abraham, Mark Scureman.

West Point's Class of 1966. Three all-American wrestlers 25 years later in 1991. L to R: Senator Bob Robbins, Col. Mark Scureman, and Bob.

Bob's welcome to Fort Richie, Maryland. Many schools and military posts welcome Bob with outdoor signs.

Family picture 1993. 1st Row: Bob, Bobbi, Ella. 2nd Row: Esther, John, Barak, Timothy. Back Row: Sarah, Eric, Keith.

Bob speaking to the student body at the Souderton Area High School in Pennsylvania.

Photo by: Christopher A. Stanley

CHAPTER

7

January 12, 1991, was a big day for fans of wrestling at Lehigh University in Bethlehem, Pennsylvania. The little college nestled snugly in the Pocono Mountain range in the Lehigh Valley has been producing top quality engineers and top quality wrestlers for over half a century. And on this occasion, wrestling supporters had come from far and near to honor the single greatest athlete in the college's proud history.

Mike Caruso compiled a record of 57-1 in his three years of varsity competition for the Engineers. He won three NCAA titles at 123 pounds, his third coming in 1967. Following graduation, he called upon the same intensity of purpose, the same drive and competitiveness which had served him so well in athletics to attain comparable success in the business world.

Inducted into the National Wrestling Hall of Fame in Stillwater, Oklahoma, just a few weeks previous, his Lehigh fans wanted to pay tribute to him in the town where he made his mark. His former coaches and teammates rolled out the superlatives in describing his career.

But one speaker provided a unique perspective. Colonel Mark Scureman had starred at West Point, one of Lehigh's arch mat rivals for bragging rights east of the Mississippi River. When Scureman took to the podium, he began in a light hearted vein, cracking jokes and quips. The crowd chuckled at his humorous remarks.

Suddenly, he turned serious. He began talking about the lone setback Caruso suffered over his entire varsity career. That setback had come at the hands of Bob Steenlage, a man who Scureman has held in the highest regard almost since the moment they first met, back in 1962.

"Not only was he my roommate, he was my best friend," Scureman told the Lehigh gathering in a solemn tone, speaking of Bob. "I was best man in his wedding, and he was best man in mine. He was a four-time state wrestling champion from Iowa, and that feat didn't get repeated for 17 more years.

"The last time I saw Bob was when I was best man at his wedding. We all went off to Vietnam in our class. There was a book written about our class; we lost more people in Vietnam than any other class at West Point. Thirty some were killed, and quite a bit more wounded." In fact, one out of every twenty cadets from that class of 1966 was killed in the Vietnam War, and one out of every six came back wounded or maimed. No other class had more killed in Vietnam than our's.

"I'll have to admit that hit Bob hard; and if you know Bob like I know Bob — he is a very sincere, very serious person," Scureman continued. "He kind of checked out of society. We didn't hear from him for many years. He had a very serious accident and almost lost his life....."

He said Bob had been invited to the event, and wanted to

attend, but couldn't. He pulled a note out of his pocket, a note which Bob had written to Caruso.

"Mike: As you know, today is a day I worked very hard to prevent. I just couldn't pull it off. I can tell you from my experiences with you a quarter of a century ago that you are a great wrestler. I can also tell you from our most recent encounters that you are just as good in the game of life. You got this honor the old fashioned way. You earned it. Congratulations. Bob Steenlage."

Mike Caruso, deeply touched by the note Scureman read, has earned all his success the hard way, it is true; and so has Bob Steenlage. Hard work, grit and determination have made him the man he is. Today, Bob and Bobbi work their farm, with six of their eight children still at home, working alongside them. They raise black Angus cattle and sheep, and grow field corn, oats and alfalfa. They have a large garden. The farm is also home to a herd of goats, many cats and a dog.

Each day begins before the crack of dawn. Once everyone is up and ready, there is a family gathering of prayer, singing and scripture reading. The farm chores follow. Everyone tends to the farm, and Bob makes his plans for travel. He is often on the phone, speaking with educators, or military and business leaders who want him to come spread his message of hope, hard work and commitment to oneself.

Sarah and Esther are looking forward to attending college soon, while Timothy, John and Barak are in the teenage years. Ella, the youngest, turned eight on August 2, 1992.

Eric, who overcame such a traumatic start — born with his skull grown together, not allowing for growth of the brain, and with a cleft lip, and after surviving the terrible car accident which sent him through the windshield — is a handsome twenty-four year old. He is a graduate of the University of Wisconsin at LaCrosse, which he attended on a Barry Goldwater Scholarship earned through high scores on an extremely competitive nationwide test. Currently he is a second-year student at Yale Medical School.

"Eric became very interested in the medical profession after all the treatment he went through," said Bob. "He liked to sit and read medical books when he was young. Then, he decided he wanted to study medicine and devote his life to helping others, just like the doctor who had operated on his head."

Keith, two years younger than Eric, graduated from vocational school in LaCrosse, as a certified diesel technician, and then decided to go to college. He brings home nearly straight A's from the University of Wisconsin at LaCrosse, and has his heart set on becoming a lawyer some day.

After all he has been through, all the mountains he has climbed, Bob Steenlage is a simple man today. He values the simple things in life the most of all.

"My favorite time of day is to be around my children, it can be any time of day," he said. "They can be doing schoolwork or chores; each day with them makes me thankful we've been on the farm because it's been a good place to raise children."

It seems now, in the winter of 1993, that Bob has finally found his calling in life. He travels the nation talking to groups comprised of educators, students, soldiers, businessmen, and athletes. His message usually begins with the statement, "I am the son of an alcoholic." It continues with stories of his troubled childhood, the challenges of West Point, the darkness of Vietnam. It ends on a very upbeat, positive note, full of hope.

Always, the emphasis is on overcoming obstacles, and on winning through hope and determination.

"I'm giving these talks because I care about young people," he said recently. "I've gone through difficult times in my own life; and I found, quite by accident, by sharing experiences with young people that they respond; they look at their own lives and say, `if that person (Bob) is willing to open up and talk about it — perhaps if I open up and talk about my problems, then maybe I can be better off with all the things I face.'"

Bob is now a man on a mission. But the mission is more complex than merely offering advice to others on how to work though problems; he is also trying to exorcise the demons of his own life, and seems well on his way to doing just that.

The first changing of his life came with the confrontation with his father in the kitchen, when in seventh grade he tried to protect his mother and was thrown into the kitchen wall.

"My mother and I sat down at the kitchen table and cried together," he recalled. "There was always so much tension in our family. I cried, `Oh God, why was I born into this horrible family situation? Why can't I have a normal family?"

That moment was, he recognized many years later, the beginning of the changing of his life. Through the emotional pain and torment, he began the process of shedding the layers of torment; it was a process that would go through several stages, and grow more intense each time.

The bitterness which Bob felt for many years toward his father came as somewhat of a surprise to his mother when it first began to pour out in the late 1980s.

"I didn't realize at the time he was growing up that he had these feelings," she said in 1993. "I knew there wasn't much contact between the two of them, and that Bob resented Jack for his drinking. But I didn't know Bob felt as strongly about it as he did."

Evelyn remembers her first husband as a man who found it difficult to express his feelings and emotions. There was six years age difference between them, and shortly after they were married Bob was conceived. Then, Jack signed up to fight in World War II and was gone from their lives for nearly two years. By the time he came home from the war, he might have been a different man. Evelyn isn't sure; time has faded many memories and many impressions. And, she didn't know a great deal about Jack before they were married. She remembers he was raised on a farm, but she's not even sure if he ever participated in any sports while attending Britt High School.

"I doubt if he did, because he was the only boy on the farm, and he probably had lots of work to do there after school," she said. "But I know he really liked football. He would try to go to most of Bob's football games, but he didn't get to very many of the wrestling matches. He didn't really know a lot about wrestling since they didn't have it when he was in school."

Evelyn remembers Jack seemed to favor their second son, Les, for whatever reason. "As a little boy, Les would jump up on Jack's lap sometimes," she recalled. "He would take Les fishing, or go to sporting events in Iowa City. But, no, I don't remember Jack every taking Bob anywhere..."

Bob was always searching for two things in his early life: acceptance from others, and a father figure. Perhaps the two were combined in the frustration he felt in the way his own father ignored him. Bob and Jack simply were never able to build a bridge of communication, for whatever reason, and that failure resulted in one of life's greatest tragedies: A son who wound up despising his father.

"I would have traded all my medals for a father and a normal family life," Bob has said over and over again. He believes there are many youngsters in America, perhaps millions of them, who share that empty feeling. "Many times, I realize young people's problems are often attributable at least partially to the home. So many young people cry out, `I hate, I hate, I hate!' — but what they really mean is, `I hurt, I hurt, I hurt!' I know what it's like to hurt and the young people sense that. They think, `If he can make it, I can make it.'"

So, his first message to the young people and to parents everywhere is to cherish and nurture the precious relationship between parent and child. It is essential for the well being of today's youth that they feel they belong to a strong family unit, that they believe they are loved and cared for. But in his travels, he sees thousands of youth who don't feel that way. His heart cracks a hundred times a month when the young students come to him after his talks, seeking advice and counseling because they are so unhappy at home.

The second part of his message is directed to all of those who feel life is almost too large to be dealt with. His message is one of hope and inspiration, one of fighting back from any adversity. One of his central themes is of a brick wall, and learning to tear it down.

"It is obvious this person has run into a brick wall, the impossible barrier," he says, speaking of anyone who has lost his way. "Is it worthwhile for this person to even try to find a way out or should he give up? In your life what `brick wall' are you now facing? It could be any of the following: A recession, your boss, any fear, a damaged family life, disabling changes in life, cutbacks at work, fierce competition.

"The key to overcoming any of these is RESPONSE - ABILITY. We have the power to choose how any problem or circumstance is going to affect us. Usually the problems control us. Responsibility in reverse is the ABILITY to choose our RESPONSE. We become a product of our values and decisions and not our moods and conditions. This simply means it isn't the problem or circumstances that defeats a person, it is how you respond.

"Then there is reaction. To REACT means there is no conscious thought process. Many of us are affected by the social environment. We often build our emotional lives around behaviors of others so weaknesses of other people control them."

"The responsibility we have is dependent upon our ability to subordinate an impulse to a value! A person must admit, `I am what I am today because of the choices I made yesterday.' What matters most in life is how we respond to what we experience.

"Another key is to be a light, not a judge; a model, not a critic; a programmer, not a program; to feed opportunities, starve problems; to keep promises and not make excuses.

"Legendary pilot Chuck Yaeger launched an era of supersonic flight on October 14, 1947, when he crashed the sound barrier and its `invincible brick wall.' Prominent scientists had no hard data that the barrier was impenetrable. Others predicted both pilot and plane would disintegrate at Mach 1, or the pilot would lose his voice, revert in age, or be severely buffeted.

"Yaeger went 700 miles per hour (Mach 1.06); three weeks later he stretched to Mach 1.35; six years later he flew at an incredible 1,612 miles per hour (Mach 2.44) putting to rest the myth of an impenetrable barrier.

"`The faster I got, the smoother the ride!' he wrote. `Suddenly, the Mach needle began to fluctuate. It went up to .965 Mach — then tipped right off the scale. I thought I was seeing things! We were flying supersonic, and it was as smooth as a baby's bottom: grandma could be sitting up there sipping lemonade. I was thunderstruck.'

"Having broken through the sound barrier, we face what many consider an even more imposing obstacle to progress — the `human barrier,'" said Bob. "For many managers today, breaking the human barrier — or status quo performance — is as difficult as breaking the sound barrier was for aeronautical engineers four decades ago.

"Why? Because people are often seen as limitations, if not liabilities, rather than advantages and assets. Thus low performance is often institutionalized in the structure and systems, procedures, and processes, of the organization. Some executives pilot their single-engine, propeller-driven firms at slow speeds and low altitudes, cocksure that anything smacking of high performance would cause them to lose control and crash.

"Meanwhile, a few well-trained and courageous managers are breaking the mythical human barrier — or brick wall — and proving that gains in human performance of 100 percent are possible without anyone losing his voice, reverting to adolescence, or experiencing violent buffeting.

"In fact, people in high-performing organizations tend to be much healthier and happier. Because they are treated as the most valuable resource of the organization, they assist each other in making quantum leaps in quality and productivity.

"We should treat both employees and customers as if they are important people. Leaders who want to grow and prosper are seeking training in the principles and practices of supersonic management and have simple faith in the soaring potential of their people.

"Training and development programs should evolve naturally from the company's vision, mission, and principles. Programs should attempt to empower people to soar, to sail, to step forward bravely into the unknown, being guided more by imagination than memory, and ultimately to reach beyond their fears and past failures.

"Sometimes we need a PUSH to overcome FEAR and bring about CHANGE — like I needed when I went to airborne school. It took me five attempts to conquer the fear of jumping out of the plane with a parachute; twice I threw up, once I crapped my pants — the first four times I needed to be prodded out the door with the help of my sergeant's boot, strategically placed on my posterior.

"There are two types of leaders: one — the do as I say type; and two, the do as I do type. You have to ask yourself which type you are.

"Before the owners of the Dallas Cowboys ever picked their first football coach, they asked the best corporations of America what was the top quality of their executives. The unanimous answer was character/integrity. The Cowboys subsequently hired a man who personified character, and Tom Landry went on to become one of the most successful and admired coaches in athletic history.

"We must change ourselves: But first we must recognize that ninety-five percent of society is negative and will never do anything about it; ninety-seven percent never set goals. But how can you work toward anything if you don't have goals?

"Finally, have you ever had a bad day? If so, think of my bad days of many years ago. The abusive father, the wrestling injuries my senior year in high school, the pressures of West Point — Vietnam, and the mine field.....

"I would like to challenge all of you who are hurting and in distress to take RESPONSIBILITY for your life and join me in running through brick walls.

"A very, very intelligent man once said, `It is the RESPONSIBILITY of every human being to aspire to do something worthwhile, to make this world a better place than the one he found. A person first starts to live when he can live outside himself, when he can have as much regard for his fellow man as he does for himself.' That man was none other than Albert Einstein."

Before finding the internal strength to accept responsibility for his life, Bob almost gave up on life himself. He admits it, and his closest friends realize it.

"Bob showed me what giving 100 percent means," said Mark Scureman, now a retired colonel. "I thought I knew, but I didn't. Nothing came easy to Bob and a lesser man would have given up many times, but not Bob. Several times I thought it was curtains for him, both at West Point and after we graduated....it got that close. But his determination, pride, hard work and love for his fellow man brought him through.

"He showed me that talent is not enough. He was the first person to show me the concept of focus. His story shows this to be true. He was my best friend and roommate at West Point. He was the best man at my wedding. I couldn't be more proud to call a man my friend."

Bob's impact on the other member of the All-American wrestling threesome was just as strong. Cindy Robbins, the wife of Senator Bob Robbins of Pennsylvania recalled in 1993 her first meeting with Bob.

"For years I had heard about a man named Bobby Steenlage," said Cindy. "My husband referred to him as not only one of his best friends and fellow classmates, but also as one of the best wrestlers to have ever come out of West Point. It wasn't until the summer of 1991 I had the opportunity to meet face to face a man I had heard so much about.

"Bob called one day out of the blue and said he was going to be in the area and wanted to stop and see us. I was delighted and made arrangements to pick him up at Edinboro University, following a motivational talk he was giving. I knew who he was the minute I saw him and in the 40 minute drive to our home I felt like I had always known him. Perhaps it was because I knew so much about him through my husband, Bob. Perhaps it was because we had so much in common or perhaps it was because Bob Steenlage is a caring, gentle person. But whatever, the reason, I knew we would become good friends too.

"My husband Bob and I have kept in close contact with Bobby and have observed him giving his speeches not only to students but to adults. We have watched his struggles in coping with the talks he was to give and have been witness to his triumphs when all has gone as it should. For a man who had such a rocky beginning, Bob is living proof of what can be accomplished if you think positively and work hard."

It took a world of positive thinking and hard work for the Steenlage family to overcome all the adversity. Love, patience, and commitment between lifetime partners was also one of the keys. But surely, the single strongest component in Bob's gallant struggle to rebound has been his faith.

"There have been some very tough times, filled with great pain....the death of two children, Eric's problems," said Bobbi. "But except for those moments, I would go through it all again. Bob and I still love each other, we have some wonderful children, and we look forward to the future together."

When asked in the winter of 1993 to sum up who he is, Bob Steenlage didn't even hesitate: "I'm a person who doesn't like to give up," he said quietly. No one who has ever met him would doubt that, for a single moment. His whole life has consisted of FIGHTING BACK.

> *"Life is a gift, and if we agree to accept it, we must contribute in return. When we fail to contribute, we fail to adequately answer why we are here."*
>
> *Albert Einstein*

Write or call:
Bob Steenlage
RR1 Box 108
Galesville, WI 54630

Call 1-800-777-8778

EPILOGUE

Since going on the road to talk to the young and the troubled people of the nation, Bob has made hundreds of friends through his inspirational and powerful message. Many of them have written to him, to offer their endorsements of his talk. Here are some of those endorsements:

*****

Mr. Bob Steenlage was a guest speaker at Ventura High School on October 22, 1992.

We all realize that we are living in an era when our language is badly inflated. A very ordinary effort can be described as `outstanding' or `great'.

Try to remember what the words excellent, superior or extraordinary used to mean, and you have described Bob Steenlage. His speech to our student body will become the benchmark against which others are measured. The assembly closed with a standing ovation!

Quality is back. Tell your neighbor!

Gary B. Schichtl, Superintendent
Ventura Community School, Ventura, Iowa

*****

This writer had the opportunity in February to hear the inspirational story of Bob Steenlage, the first four-time state champion in Iowa history. Bob tells his story to elementary, junior high and high school students all over the country. It is an inspirational story of abuse and rejection at the hands of an alcoholic father and the effects that supportive teachers and coaches can have in saving youngsters from the results of such a life. It is a story of how a young person who is dedicated to achieving a goal can overcome insurmountable odds if there are people willing to lend support. And it is a story of the pain and emotional scars caused by the abuse of alcohol.

A few issues back we recommended Jeff Blatnick, 1984 Olympic Gold Medalist, as a speaker for any type of event. Now we give you another wrestling hero who is an excellent speaker and representative of the sport. For talks on topics ranging from motivation to suicide or the Vietnam experience, contact Bob Steenlage at RR 1, Box 108, Galesville, Wisconsin 54630. His phone is 1-800-777-8778.

Cal Johnson, Assistant Editor
Wrestling U.S.A.

*****

Thank you for your recent talk here at Douglas County High School. After my daughter heard you speak earlier in the week, she urged me to come listen to your second presentation at Douglas County High School. I gave up a fishing trip with my husband to hear your talk and see what she was so enthused about.

I was glad to hear so much wisdom pouring out to our high school students. Please keep up the good work. Your talk was one of the better things our school district has done for our young people.

And yes, it was well worth missing the fishing trip for — and I love to go fishing.

Rita Rogers, parent, Castle Rock, Colorado

*****

I am writing on behalf of Bob Steenlage and his powerful presentation to young people. I contracted Mr. Steenlage to speak to students at our high school, middle school, five elementaries, and to our wrestlers. It was my privilege to witness these presentations.

I was a bit concerned that he would not be able to hold the attention of our middle and high school students. To my surprise, he not only held their attention, but touched many of our students emotions. In the seventeen years I have been in our district, I do not ever recall a speaker receiving a standing ovation at the high school — Bob Steenlage did!

His presentation is one that quickly gets a listener's attention, and soon grabs them by the heart. I was amazed that it wasn't just certain individuals that were being affected by his messages. Everyone seemed to be awed by his story. His delivery was forceful, but his humble manner added to his effectiveness.

At the elementary level, he quickly captured the children's attention. His presentations, understandable, is not as direct and forceful as that of his secondary presentation. However, because of his demeanor, his point was well made and understood. In my estimation his elementary presentation was age appropriate and very well done.

We were honored to have Bob Steenlage speak to the students in our school district. It is without equivocation that I would recommend him as a speaker. I feel our students were inspired and motivated by his presentations.

> Beth Frye, Drug-Free School Coordinator,
> School District No. Re-1, Sterling, Colorado

*****

Bob Steenlage was a classmate of mine at West Point; a fellow wrestling team member and one of my best friends during our college years. For several years now, Bob has been traveling throughout the country giving drug and alcohol/motivational talks at high schools and colleges, for clubs and corporations. He has a message that can reach people of all ages, from all walks of life. Bob's speech is inspiring and uplifting because he's been at the bottom and through sheer determination, overcame what most would call insurmountable odds.

I feel confident Bob would be an ideal speaker for an assembly at your school to help the youth of Pennsylvania understand they can overcome any obstacles if they set goals and strive to reach them.

Robert D. Robbins, State Senator of Pennsylvania

*****

As a member of the Goodhue Community Drug Prevention Committee, I had the privilege of meeting and introducing Mr. Bob Steenlage to students at Goodhue High School. He spoke to students on both the elementary and secondary levels during the day and to parents in an evening presentation in conjunction with parent-teacher conferences.

Mr. Steenlage's presentation, taken directly from his own experiences, challenges and encourages people at all levels to make good choices, learn from life's experiences — both negative and positive — and challenge themselves to do their very best through goal setting and determined commitment to those goals.

As a former teacher, I was impressed with Mr. Steenlage's sensitivity to the various age levels, and his ability to adapt his message to his audience. His presentation was clear, matter-of-fact and compelling as he described his life as the son of an abusive and alcoholic father, as the "skinny kid" not expected to achieve athletic recognition, the student told he was "too dumb" to go to college, and the disillusioned Vietnam vet.

Because of Mr. Steenlage's wide range of experience and expertise, his message is adaptable to a number of audiences, and is effective in each setting. He is able to challenge young people to resist drugs and alcohol; he is able to speak to athletes about overcoming the odds; he is able to speak to those who must accept academic limitations, admitting that he was near the bottom of his West Point class; and he is able to speak to parents about their responsibility to their children. In all of these areas I would highly recommend him. His message to each of these groups is: Success can be achieved despite obstacles. He urged individuals to look inward, set goals, make a commitment to reach the goals and never give up.

Mr. Steenlage has an impressive ability to hold a student audience. He uses an educational approach, gives honest answers to questions and shows genuine interest in helping kids and their parents. Most of all, he leaves his audiences of all ages with a great deal of hope and encouragement. It's a message sorely needed in our schools.

Student reaction following Monday's presentation was very favorable. Students with whom I spoke were impressed with his story, believing him to be genuine and his message reliable. I highly recommend Mr. Steenlage as a speaker and found him to be an unusually warm, caring person.

Millie Mehrkens, Goodhue Editor, The News
Goodhue, Minnesota

*****

Mr. Steenlage: I had the privilege of hearing your presentation to the Colby public. Your story of setting a goal and staying with it, no matter what, gives encouragement to parents as well as students to pursue and strive for good things in life. The difficulties you have overcome show it is not an easy path to live a life with high values and morals, but that it is very worthwhile.

Your soft-spoken style gives an atmosphere of confidence and a gentle, fatherly image of someone who really cares. Because you have endured through difficult situations in family and with people in your life, students, as well as adults, know you are real and they can share their hurts with you knowing you will understand.

Our country surely needs the positive attitude you present towards children and the encouragement you give to parents today. You give students a purpose to strive for the best they can do and not look too intently at anyone's opinion of them. You enforce parents to fully take on their job as a parent with all their heart because their children are worth every minute of effort to direct their lives into adulthood with a good image of themselves.

Thank you for stressing accountability for each person, of and in themselves, as something that all can take on and live to be the best they can without being pulled down by social pressure.

Your wisdom and care are confirmed in the questions and answer time, as you weigh each question in your mind and answer in love, giving direction to benefit the life of those who inquired.

Mr. Steenlage, thank you for caring so much to be willing to give so much of yourself to make America a better future for all Americans.

Connie Mullins, School Board Member
Colby, Wisconsin

*****

I wish to express my deep gratitude for your coming to Walcott Junior High to speak to our student body. The students were more attentive to your presentations than any school assembly I have seen in the past twenty years. Many students and faculty came to me with positive remarks about your program. You certainly had a positive influence on the lives of our young people. You were the topic of conversation the next day.

Many adults will name a teacher who had a positive influence on their lives. The experience we share is the reverse. As a student, you had a powerful influence on my life. When I came to Britt during your sophomore year, I was fascinated by your work ethics and accomplishments. Seemingly, without the ability, you accomplished goals most people only dream about.

You continue to fascinate me. I don't understand how anyone can stand before a large group of junior high students and hold their attention, but you can do it — with a powerful, positive message.

I hope you get back to the Quad Cities next year and speak in some of our schools that you weren't able to visit on this trip. More kids need to hear your story. We give our kids too many excuses for not doing well. Its nice to hear how someone turned negative influences into positive motivation. Thanks for coming to Walcott.

> Bob LeMar, Counselor, Davenport Community School
> District, Walcott Schools, Iowa

*****

Dear Mr. Steenlage: Wanted to write and thank you for your presentations to our students and parents. All three presentations were excellent!

I especially appreciated the session with our parents/community patrons on Wednesday night. You were very open and honest in sharing your experiences and beliefs about the role of parents in the development of their children. It is my belief that the message you bring to students is excellent, but the message to parents is even better. I would encourage you to pursue this avenue at other schools as well. All schools should plan a session for you to speak with parents.

> Kevin W. Fiene, Principal, Community Schools
> Denver, Iowa

*****

I would highly recommend Bob Steenlage as an inspirational speaker for any group. His presentation to our student body of adjudicated delinquent youth was outstanding and he held their complete attention. Students even stayed afterward to talk to Bob because his message so closely related to experiences they had undergone in their own lives. Most importantly, he left our group with the dream that they too can be a success in life and that no circumstance is too large to overcome.

He gave a big lift to all of our student body.

Steven R. Huston, Superintendent, State Training School,
Eldora, Iowa

*****

I heard Bob Steenlage deliver his "I am a Son" talk to the student body and faculty at Waynedale High School, Applecreek, Ohio last spring.

In my 46 years of experience in coaching and teaching in the Ohio Public Schools and the College of Wooster, I have never heard a more inspirational speaker. Long after the talk was ended the students remained in the auditorium and participated in an informal questions and answer session.

Bob Steenlage speaks with power and warmth. He is tops in developing rapport with youth.

Phil Shipe, Professional Emeritus
College of Wooster, Ohio

*****

Picture an auditorium filled with sleepy-eyed teenagers unknowingly preparing to hear a message that could change the entire course of their lives. Enter Bob Steenlage, a seemingly humble man, whose message resounds loudly and clearly to every individual in attendance.

For those struggling with parental abuse, low self- esteem, dysfunctional families, alcohol or drug dependence, he offers a message of hope.

The audience remains captivated as he retells the story of his incredibly difficult life as the child of an abusive, alcoholic father, who seemed to have all the chances for success against him. He was thrown his first lifeline, he feels, by a teacher/coach/mentor who guided him through his difficult struggles to become a four-time state wrestling champion. As the story of his life unfolds, his achievements become even more inspirational.

All who leave their seats after hearing Bob's message have been motivated in some way. For some it may give them the courage to say NO to their next drink; for others it may set the groundwork to achieve a livelong goal of becoming the very best that each of us can be.

His message is unassuming, yet powerful. Don't miss the opportunity to hear Bob Steenlage!

Robert B. Beaumont, Assistant Principal
James Buchanan High School, Mercersburg, Pennsylvania

****

As an administrator at Indian Valley Middle School, may I first express my sincere thanks to you for recently coming to eastern Pennsylvania during which time you reached out to over five thousand students in the Souderton Area School District by sharing your motivational message in each of the district's elementary and secondary schools.

Having conducted an extensive background check prior to your arrival, I can now confirm first-hand my unprecedented findings — namely, that your powerful delivery and timely message are indeed extraordinary and second to none in motivating or meeting the needs of today's youth. After captivating their attention for an hour, our students came away with a clear notion that they too can overcome "insurmountable" odds by making right choices, setting personal goals, and then settling for nothing less than their best efforts — echoing your personal standard of "Do something poorly until you can do it well, but get started."

Likewise, they extracted from your personal story that

unless there is a forgiving spirit within each of us, the healing of emotional wounds is not likely to occur.

Bob, not only did I enjoy having you as a guest in my home, I also received a great deal of personal satisfaction acting as a coordinator in setting up thirty separate assembly programs within nine surrounding school districts during your two-week stay. Since then, I have received many individual expressions of appreciation from students, teachers, administrators, support staff, and parents of all school levels — persons who genuinely appreciated your ability to personally touch their lives as well as the dramatic and forceful way you were able to weave a tale of personal tragedy into one of hope and triumph. One can only encourage you to continue pressing on with your story of Fighting Back and being a winner.

All student's in America's schools today need to hear your inspiring message of overcoming obstacles — whether that obstacle be one of dealing with a dysfunctional family, substance abuse, suicide, peer pressure, or personal tragedy. Today, there are many young students in both public and private schools who walk around in silence with deep wounds carefully screened, and who better than you, a man who has hit bottom and overcome tragedy at every state of his life, can understand a student in crisis as well as give that child or individual the courage to expose his/her inner turmoil and deal with it. Because of your direct, honest, and empathetic approach in effectively dealing with our schools' children, it is understandable why you have rapidly become one of our nation's most sought-after speakers.

J. Harold Zook, Assistant Principal
Indian Valley Middle School, Harleysville, Pennsylvania

*****

To whom it may concern: I had the opportunity to attend a seminar at Ft. Ritchie Maryland on December 7, 1992. The seminar was the kickoff for Alcohol and Drug Awareness Week at Ft. Ritchie.

The guest speaker for the event was Mr. Bob Steenlage from Galesville, Wisconsin. His presentation was excellent and carried the theme of "Response—Ability". He talked about events in his life and how his determination made him who he is today. His presentation had the audience laughing one minute and in tears the next.

Mr. Steenlage was entertaining, motivational, inspirational, and thought provoking during the entire seminar. He explained how each of us has the unique ability to respond in many ways to a given situation. He stated that individuals must accept the responsibility for their actions and decisions. His message was clear and concise reiterating that adults must set an example for our young people of tomorrow.

Mr. Steenlage is a great motivational speaker and I would recommend his presentation to any audience from grade school children to corporate executives.

Joseph O. Evenstad, Major
Office of the Surgeon General
Department of the Army, Falls Church, Virginia

*****

Dear Mr. Steenlage: I wish to take this opportunity to express my sincere appreciation for your outstanding efforts associated with the National Drunk and Drugged Driving Awareness Campaign at Red River Army Depot, Texarkana, Texas.

The message on how you overcame life's obstacles and triumph over adversity to become a winner was uplifting and encouraging. The secrets you offered for motivation and success are valuable goals for each individual to strive for in their lives.

Your dedication to visiting schools across the country telling youth how they can overcome the influence of drugs, alcohol, and peer pressure is commendable. Your contribution to this work is an inspiration and encouragement to the employees of Red River Army Depot. May God continue to bless you and your family.

Thomas Dunn, Colonel, U. S. Army Commanding Officer
Department of the Army, Red River Army Depot
Texarkana, Texas

*****

Just a note to say "Thanks" in a **BIG** way for an excellent presentation last week at our Activities Eligibility meeting. Your talk was very frank and to the point, and I doubt there were any dry eyes in the auditorium when you were finished. Your experiences showed our students and parents the importance of commitment, goal-setting, overcoming adversity, and parental support. The icing on the cake for us was the introduction of your mother. Wow! Talk about a tug at the heart-strings!

You are to be commended for overcoming those struggles in your life, and I know you will be very successful in assisting kids as they experience many of those struggles in their own lives. I can easily recommend your talk to all schools.

Enclosed is a copy of the tape you requested. We had to make several copies because of requests from parents not able to attend.

Again, thanks for everything. If I can be of any help to you, do not hesitate.

Dan Conrad, Principal,Webster City, Iowa

Write or call:
Bob Steenlage
RR1 Box 108
Galesville, WI 54630

Call 1-800-777-8778

About the Author

Fighting Back is Mike Chapman's tenth book. His articles have appeared in 17 national magazines and he has won numerous awards for his writing. Mike has been selected National Wrestling Writer of the Year four times. Currently, he is managing editor of The Telegraph newspaper in Dixon, Illinois. He and his wife, Bev, have three children: Jacquie, Jenny and Jason.